First World War
and Army of Occupation
War Diary
France, Belgium and Germany

46 DIVISION
Divisional Troops
17 Sanitary Section
21 August 1916 - 7 December 1916

WO95/2681/3

The Naval & Military Press Ltd
www.nmarchive.com
Published in association with The National Archives

Published by

The Naval & Military Press Ltd

Unit 10 Ridgewood Industrial Park,

Uckfield, East Sussex,

TN22 5QE England

Tel: +44 (0) 1825 749494

www.naval-military-press.com

www.nmarchive.com

This diary has been reprinted in facsimile from the original. Any imperfections are inevitably reproduced and the quality may fall short of modern type and cartographic standards.

© Crown Copyright
Images reproduced by permission of The National Archives, London, England, 2015.

Contents

Document type	Place/Title	Date From	Date To
Miscellaneous	Recommendation for all Kitchens & Cookhouses of the Division. Including Officers and Sergeants Mess Kitchens. Appendix A		
Heading	46 Div 17 San Sect 1916 Aug-1917 Mar To 3 Army		
War Diary	Bavincourt	23/08/1916	24/08/1916
War Diary	Bavincourt	04/10/1916	31/10/1916
Miscellaneous	Bavincourt	25/08/1916	28/08/1916
War Diary	Bavincourt	21/08/1916	23/08/1916
War Diary		23/10/1916	31/10/1916
Miscellaneous	Bavincourt	20/08/1916	21/08/1916
War Diary		06/10/1917	20/10/1917
War Diary	Bavincourt	29/08/1916	28/02/1917
War Diary		13/02/1917	26/09/1917
Miscellaneous		12/09/1917	12/09/1917
War Diary	St. Riquier	06/11/1916	11/11/1916
Miscellaneous	Plan of Kitchen Table		
War Diary	Hinu.	01/03/1917	08/03/1917
War Diary	Lucheux	01/12/1916	22/12/1916
War Diary	Henie	08/03/1917	31/12/1917
Miscellaneous		15/12/1916	16/12/1916
Miscellaneous	Henu.	22/03/1917	31/03/1917
War Diary	Henu.	13/03/1917	30/03/1917
War Diary	Henu.	01/02/1917	20/02/1917
War Diary	Gouy.	20/02/1917	20/02/1917
War Diary	Henu.	17/03/1917	21/03/1917
Diagram etc	Down-Draught Incinerator at Drying Room Pommier. Appendix A.		
Miscellaneous			
War Diary		23/03/1917	28/03/1917
War Diary		06/12/1917	14/12/1917
War Diary		04/01/1917	31/01/1917
War Diary		17/12/1917	31/12/1917
War Diary		19/12/1917	19/12/1917
War Diary		05/02/1917	05/02/1917
War Diary		03/02/1917	13/02/1917
Miscellaneous			
War Diary		03/01/1917	04/01/1917
War Diary		20/12/1917	24/12/1917
War Diary		13/01/1917	19/01/1917
War Diary		17/01/1917	21/01/1917
Miscellaneous			
War Diary	Henu.	01/01/1917	02/01/1917
War Diary		04/12/1917	06/12/1917
War Diary		10/01/1917	12/01/1917
Diagram etc	Plan and Section of Scheme for disposal of Excreta Appendix B		
Diagram etc	Pedestal Urinals Appendix C.		
War Diary	Bavincourt	30/08/1916	31/08/1916
War Diary	Henu.	07/12/1916	07/12/1916

Diagram etc	Townson & Mercer's Monthly Meteorological Record. Appendix C		
Miscellaneous			
Diagram etc	Appendix A		
Miscellaneous		26/03/1917	26/03/1917
War Diary	Henu.	00/01/1917	00/01/1917
Diagram etc	Townson & Mercer's Monthly Meteorological Record.		
Miscellaneous	Flyproof Box Latrine Seat For Use With Buckets Or Deep Trench		
Diagram etc	Townson & Mercer's Monthly Meteorological Record. Appendix "C".		
Diagram etc	Townson & Mercer's Monthly Meteorological Record. Appendix H		
Diagram etc	Townson & Mercer's Monthly Meteorological Record.		
Diagram etc	Deep Trench Latrine Flyproof Cover.		
Miscellaneous	Report on Water Supplies for Gommecourt Appendix B		
Diagram etc	Townson & Mercer's Monthly Meteorological Record.		
Miscellaneous	Water Report.		
Miscellaneous	Report on Battn. Gommecourt.	22/03/1917	22/03/1917
Diagram etc	Townson & Mercer's Monthly Meteorological Record. Appendix F.		
Miscellaneous	Town Major Lucheux Appendix B.		
Miscellaneous	R.A.M.C. Circular Memorandum No. 81 Appendix B.		
Miscellaneous	A.D.M.S. 46 Division	23/12/1916	23/12/1916
Miscellaneous	O/C Trench Mission. 46th Division. Appendix G		
Miscellaneous	D.D.M.S. Vth Corps Report on Water Supplies at Fonquevillers, Gommecourt and Essarts. Appendix C		
Miscellaneous		29/11/1916	29/11/1916
Miscellaneous	Town Major Lucheux	01/12/1916	01/12/1916
Miscellaneous	A.D.M.S. 46th N.M. Division. Appendix F.		
Miscellaneous	O.C., Regt. Appendix D.	21/01/1917	21/01/1917
Miscellaneous	A.D.M.S. 46th Division Appendix C.	07/01/1917	07/01/1917
Diagram etc	Spot Map. Civilian Cases of Measles. Appendix E		
Diagram etc	Sketch Plan of Old German Baths Gommecourt Appendix E.		
Miscellaneous		23/01/1917	23/01/1917
Miscellaneous	A.D.M.S. 46 Division	23/12/1916	23/12/1916
Miscellaneous	To:- Town Major	07/12/1916	07/12/1916
Miscellaneous			
Diagram etc	Drawings of Drying Room and Incinerator existing. on site of 3rd N.M. Field Ambulance at Gaudiempre. Scale 1/4 Inch to 1 Foot. Appendix A.		
Miscellaneous	Water Report	09/03/1917	09/03/1917
Miscellaneous		26/01/1917	26/01/1917
Miscellaneous		10/01/1917	10/01/1917
Heading	No. 46 Div. Sanitary Section August 1916		
Heading	(No 17) 46th Divisional Sanitary Section Feb. 1917		
Heading	WO95/2681/3		
Heading	46th Division 17th Sanitary Section Oct 1916		
Heading	46th Division 17th Sanitary Section Jan. 1917		
Miscellaneous	(No.17) 46th Divl Sanitary Section. Nov 1916		
Miscellaneous	No. 46th Divl. Sanitary Section. Sept. 1916.		
Heading	46th Div. No. 17. Sanitary Section Mar. 1917.		
Miscellaneous	(no 17) 46th Divl. Sanitary Section. Dec. 1916		
Miscellaneous			

Appendix A

Recommendations for all Kitchens & Cookhouses of the Division
including Officers' and Sergeants' Mess Kitchens.

1. Attention is directed to R.A.M.C. Routine Order No. 83 dated 6/8/16 circulated already. These recommendations should be put into practice at once.

2. **Personnel**
   (a) None of the personnel should be allowed to sleep in the kitchen. If it is essential for one man to sleep in it to look after stores, his bedding, etc, should be removed early in the morning for cleansing, before the preparation of food begins.
   (b) Cooks should be as clean as any man in the Unit.
   (c) No one except the men actually employed there should be allowed to enter the kitchens.
   (d) No clothes should be kept in them.

3. All floors, tables, shelves, etc, should be scrubbed at least once a day with a dilute solution of Cresol, and the walls sprayed two or three times a day with the same solution, to keep down the flies.

4. All cutlery, choppers, frying pans, etc, should be kept clean with a solution of soda (obtained from Ordnance).

5. A kitchen or cookhouse, if properly attended to, should always bear inspection at any hour of the day.

6. **Care of Food**
   Except in the trenches, food should be kept in safes. It is thought that a collapsible form of safe might be manufactured at any rate for Infantry Units, by the Brigade workshops.
   In the trenches petrol tins with one side perforated with fine holes, with a French nail, should be used. The holes should not be large enough to admit a house fly.
   Large articles of food should be kept, in the trenches, in clean wood boxes with lids of gauze on frames. The frames should fit accurately over the sides of the boxes.
   All these receptacles for food should be scrubbed out frequently.

7. Cooks must be held responsible for the condition of grease traps, sinks, etc, belonging to their cookhouse and kitchens.

8. The sites for cookhouses and kitchens should, in so far as it is possible, be selected. The windows of these institutions should not overlook dung pits and manure heaps.

9. The cookhouses & kitchens of the Division are often found to be dirty on inspection, and the cooks are nearly always so. Officers' kitchens are the principal offenders.
The Third Army have asked for a sanitary inspection of all kitchens and cookhouses, as the result of criticisms of D.A.D.M.S. Sanitation Third Army.
It is hoped an improvement will soon be evident.

10. It is recommended that paras. 2, 3, 4, 5, 6 & 7 or orders framed on them should be placed in every cookhouse & kitchen of the Division.

11. The least disastrous result of neglect of kitchens would be a serious outbreak of Diarrhoea, of which disease there have been a good number of cases in the Division lately.

46 DIV

17 SAN SECT

1916 AUG — 1917 MAR

~~B~~ ~~2504~~

To 3 ARMY

WAR DIARY
or
INTELLIGENCE SUMMARY

Army Form C. 2118.

Place	Date	Hour	Summary of Events and Information	Remarks and references to Appendices
BAVINCOURT	23/8/16		When any recruits arrive for them to perform the duties of nature they should. The ground and collect the nuisance complained of. He arranged with the Sergeant Major of the Labour Battalion to clean up all the foules found and in future to dig short latrines near the place where the men were working and keep them in a sanitary state. In the afternoon I attended to office work. I visited my Sergeant in charge of a detachment at BAILLEULMONT and another Sergeant in charge of a detachment at LA CAUCHIE to arrange about the disinfection of the dugouts and shelters in the trenches which I have previously reported. Twenty men from the 2nd N.M. Field Ambulance were apprentices to the R.E.C. placed under my R.C.O.	
Do	24/8/16		In the afternoon I attended to office work and visited with the D.A.D.M.S. and Q.M.S. Lieut King (3rd N.M. Field Ambulance) The town Major at LA CAUCHIE to arrange for accommodation for treating and disinfecting 700 N.Y.D contact cases. It was decided to allot 4 huts on the LAHERLIERE — LA CAUCHIE road for this purpose	

3/-

MEDICAL

Army Form C. 2118.

46 D[th] Secretary

47 Secretary

WAR DIARY
or
INTELLIGENCE SUMMARY

(Erase heading not required.)

Instructions regarding War Diaries and Intelligence Summaries are contained in F. S. Regs., Part II. and the Staff Manual respectively. Title pages will be prepared in manuscript.

Hour, Date, Place	Summary of Events and Information	Remarks and references to Appendices
BAVINCOURT OCTOBER 4th 1916	On being informed that an epidemic of Scarlet Fever had broken out among the 5th North Staffords, I paid a visit to the Battalion and found the following. On September 28th a man was sent to the Field Ambulance where he was diagnosed as a suspected case of Scarlet Fever. On October 3rd 4th and 5th that more cases were sent away all of whom turned out to be Scarlet Fever. 100 men who have been in contact with the above and belonged to the Battalion Headquarters Coy and some Officers servants were strictly isolated in one billet and a hut. They had separate kitchens, latrines etc, and only left the billet to go out marching. The isolation was complete, and at the end	

Hour, Date, Place	Summary of Events and Information	Remarks and references to Appendices
October 31st	This Brigade and the 236th are both now fully equipped with these sanitary appliances. During the month the deep pickled latrine in the left sector of the Brincks has been used. I describe the methods employed in my War Diary of last month. It was found that the found was too permeable to hold sufficient liquid to form a septic tank. I have suggested that where a other trench is made, a wooden trench of rough wood should be placed at the bottom of the trench so as to form a receptacle to hold liquid material. The oil could then be placed on this liquid material and an anaerobic septic tank formed. With reference to the dry-boxes as I described	

7

Army Form C. 2118.

WAR DIARY
or
INTELLIGENCE SUMMARY
(Erase heading not required.)

Instructions regarding War Diaries and Intelligence Summaries are contained in F. S. Regs., Part II. and the Staff Manual respectively. Title Pages will be prepared in manuscript.

Place	Date	Hour	Summary of Events and Information	Remarks and references to Appendices
BAVINCOURT	25/8/16		Subject the greater part of the morning in the trenches of the 5 Leicester Sub-Sector and arranged for the dugouts and shelters to be disinfected. Also arranged with the Town Major of BIENVILLERS for the accommodation of 20 men and one dying to carry out the disinfection. I was accompanied by Serjeant Cross the R.E.O. in the charge of LA CAUCHIE Subsector.	
Do	26/8/16		I attended to office work and lectures in the afternoon at the School of Sanitation.	
Do	27/8/16		I visited BONNIER and BIENVILLERS to ascertain if the fatigue party from the 2nd N.M. Field Ambulance has commenced the work of disinfection. I found they had arrived without steel helmets and were ordered by the 138 Brigade Staff to obtain Steel Helmets and not to commence work until they had Steel Helmets. These were procured the next day.	
Do	28/8/16		I visited BIENVILLERS in the morning and found the fatigue party had gone to the trenches and commenced working. In the afternoon I lectured at the School of Sanitation and attended to office work 4	

WAR DIARY
or
INTELLIGENCE SUMMARY

Army Form C. 2118.

Place	Date	Hour	Summary of Events and Information	Remarks and references to Appendices
BAVINCOURT	21/3/16		The sanitation of POMMIER. I also visited the 4th Lincolns at BIENVILLERS, saw the R.M.O. and C.O. Visited the Town Major of BIENVILLERS with them and arranged for the cleaning of streets and billets unoccupied by troops. In the afternoon I returned and lectured at the School of Sanitation and finished my office work.	
Do	22/3/16		I spent the morning attending to office work and visited the School of Sanitation. In the afternoon I lectured and attended to office work.	
Do	23/3/16		I received a complaint about the tanks of a stream and some horses rows at COULLEMONT which were being fouled by some unknown person. Some Indian Cavalry had just been billeted in this village, and it was thought that it was setting a very bad example to native troops. I visited the Town Major at COULLEMONT and he & I went to interview the Commanding Officer of the Indian Cavalry. We found ——— on investigation that a party of the Labour Battalion who were stationed at HUMBERCOURT, were working on the road and	

Army Form C. 2118.

WAR DIARY
or
INTELLIGENCE SUMMARY.
(Erase heading not required.)

Instructions regarding War Diaries and Intelligence Summaries are contained in F.S. Regs., Part II. and the Staff Manual respectively. Title pages will be prepared in manuscript.

Hour, Date, Place	Summary of Events and Information	Remarks and references to Appendices
	Billets in the villages occupied by the troops who had been in the trenches. I advised the 139th Brigade and arranged for 10 men to come into spray with 3% solution of formalin all dugouts billets in BAILLEULVAL, BASSEUX, BELLACOURT, GROSVILLE, BRETINCOURT. It took three days to complete these villages.	
October 23rd	I arranged with the 137th Brigade to have all their billets sprayed out in a similar manner which was done in BAILLEULMONT and BERLES. It was my intention to include the 138th Brigade in this desinfection but I was ordered to return the fatigue party to their units & leave	
October 30th	The Division was moving to another area. I supplied the 232nd Brigade R.F.A. with carbolic oil drums and spraying coats.	

WAR DIARY
or
INTELLIGENCE SUMMARY.
(Erase heading not required.)

Army Form C. 2118.

Hour, Date, Place	Summary of Events and Information	Remarks and references to Appendices
October 31st	During the month ending today there have been 25 cases of Infectious Disease. Diphtheria 14 cases 1.3.9th Bde Machine Gun Coy — 1 5th Lincolns — 2 8th Nottsand Derby — 1 4th Lincolns — 6 6th Notts and Derby — 1 5th Leicesters — 1 5th Staff: ord Regt — 1 5th North Staffs — 1 The majority of these have occurred among the 4th Lincolns. This battalion is being examined for carriers. up to the present 2? that ? 13 have been found. These are sent to the field Ambulance and if swabs from their throats show a positive reaction after two weeks they are evacuated to a C.C.S. Scarlet fever 4 cases all in the 5th North Staffords	

10

MEDICAL

WAR DIARY
or
INTELLIGENCE SUMMARY

Army Form C. 2118.

46 D Sanitary
See Vol 1

Place	Date	Hour	Summary of Events and Information	Remarks and references to Appendices
BAVINCOURT	20/8/16		I received a communication from the D.A.D.M.S. of the 46th Division requiring me to keep a War Diary. When this question arose over a year ago, The A.D.M.S. of this division decided that it was not necessary for me to keep it, and that anything of interest during the month when discussed over the Tel. to him and he would include it in his diary. I have advised this and considered the question settled.
Do.	21/8/16		During this morning I visited the village of POMMIER and had a discussion with Lieut Hutchinson of the 138th Brigade Office who represented the Brigade Major and attended the Sanitary Station. He arranged about the disinfection of the dugouts and shelters in the Leicester and Lincoln outpost of the trenches. It was arranged that a Sergeant R.A.M.C. of my section should superintend the fumigation with formalin vapour of the dugouts which could be made air-tight and the spraying with formalin of all the other dugouts and open shelters. I visited the town traps and disposed

WAR DIARY
or
INTELLIGENCE SUMMARY.
(Erase heading not required.)

Army Form C. 2118.

Instructions regarding War Diaries and Intelligence Summaries are contained in F. S. Regs., Part II. and the Staff Manual respectively. Title pages will be prepared in manuscript.

Hour, Date, Place	Summary of Events and Information	Remarks and references to Appendices
October 6th & 7th	Visited the Town Major of the villages which belong to this area and arranged that a N.C.O. should be allotted to each village who was to work under the Town Major. His duties were:- (1) To inspect the village (2) To report on the state of the roads. (3) To report on any insanitary conditions found in the village. (4) To report on the state of billets left by units. (5) To report on vacant billets. (6) To inspect wells and report on their condition (7) To supervise fatigue parties working on the roads, cleaning billets, attending to public urinals, latrines and abluted benches	

WAR DIARY
or
INTELLIGENCE SUMMARY.
(Erase heading not required.)

Army Form C. 2118.

Hour, Date, Place	Summary of Events and Information	Remarks and references to Appendices
October 9th	It was found necessary to allot a Sanitary squad to those villages where Battalions were not stationed as difficulties arose over procuring the necessary men for fatigues. Each Sanitary squad consists of 4 Light duty men from the Field Ambulances and are paid as Govt. MONCHIET, BAVINCOURT, SAULTY, COULLEMONT & LA BRETOILE & LA HERLIERE. I supplied the 230th Brigade R.F.A. with 17 Oil drums and fly traps and for latrines 20 Incinerator buckets have not seen any more fly traps in a satisfactory condition. I hope by supplying the above oil drums, it would help prevent fly recruitation.	
October 20th	After the visit of the D.A.D.M.S (San) 3rd Army it was thought desirable to disinfect all	

WAR DIARY
or
INTELLIGENCE SUMMARY.
(Erase heading not required.)

Army Form C. 2118.

Hour, Date, Place	Summary of Events and Information	Remarks and references to Appendices
	Last month 2½ in Appendix B of my War Diary. The R.M.O. of the 5-5 Cheshires smelter complete. The work and it was being used when we left the area. The same Medical Officer I have made some tables for the kitchens of this battalion. They are made of ordinary wood 4'×1'6" and lined with tin from two biscuit tins forming the tops. These are joined together described below and a little solder run onto the joins. The surface formed is perfectly smooth and there are no crevices or holes for dirt and grease to collect in.	

Army Form C. 2118.

WAR DIARY
or
INTELLIGENCE SUMMARY.
(Erase heading not required.)

Instructions regarding War Diaries and Intelligence Summaries are contained in F. S. Regs., Part II and the Staff Manual respectively. Title pages will be prepared in manuscript.

Hour, Date, Place	Summary of Events and Information	Remarks and references to Appendices

of 8 days as no further cases occurred the men were allowed to return to their duties. I made the following report to the A.D.M.S.

To :- A.D.M.S.
46 Division

Reference to Regular fever in the 1/5 North Stafford

I visited Baillonmont and found the following had been evacuated from this Unit

(1) Sept 28. :- Pte COOPER
(2) Oct. 4. " Pte GRIFFITH
(3) Oct. 4. " Pte TUNSTALL
(4) " 5. " Pte PLANT
(5) " 5. " Pte DOWNING

Cases 2, 3, and 4 were contacts of No 1. The contacts of the first 4 cases amount to 47 men and 4 officers. These are being

2/

(73989) W4141—463. 400,000. 9/14. H.&J.Ltd. Forms/C. 2118/10.

Army Form C. 2118.

WAR DIARY
or
INTELLIGENCE SUMMARY.
(Erase heading not required.)

Hour, Date, Place	Summary of Events and Information	Remarks and references to Appendices
5/6/6	rigidly isolated for 8 days. There are 60 contacts from the 3rd Case which are also being strictly isolated. The 107 men are isolated in their billets and have their own kitchens and sanitary arrangements. The four officers are also strictly isolated in their own billets. All medical officers are examining all contacts twice a day and also the billets are being disinfected with formalin spray. There have been no cases of this disease in Bailleulmont since we came here. Signed H.K. Parbury, Lieut. R.A.M.C. Sanitary Section 46 Division	

WAR DIARY or INTELLIGENCE SUMMARY

Army Form C. 2118.

Place	Date	Hour	Summary of Events and Information	Remarks and references to Appendices
BAVINCOURT	29/8/16		The D.M.S. of the 3rd Army visited and inspected the School of Sanitation. He was accompanied by the C.O. School of Sanitation, D.A.D.M.S. (San.) Third Army, A.D.M.S. 46th Division, D.A.D.M.S. 46th Division and myself. After the inspection the A.D.M.S. visited the Trenches of the Leicester and Leicester Regt. and inspected the Sanitation of the dug-outs. The spraying of the shelters seem to have been carried out without any difficulty but the fumigation by formalin vapour does not seem to have been very successful. Some of the lamps did not seem to have blued and the exposures were not sufficiently airtight. The fumes of the formalin were kept in the dug-outs where such-and-such for 4 hours. The standard most of the day in the trenches and arrived here about forming rain too late to give my lecture at the School of Sanitation.	
Do	30/8/16		I spent the whole of the day in the trenches of the North and South Staffords examining the dug-outs and arranging for	

WAR DIARY
or
INTELLIGENCE SUMMARY.
(Erase heading not required.)

Army Form C. 2118.

Hour, Date, Place	Summary of Events and Information	Remarks and references to Appendices
	Measles 2 cases in the following units 46 Sant Staffs Column - 1 4th Lincolns - 1 3 cases the following units Typhoid Fever in the following units 6th North Staffords - 2 5th North Staffords - 1 Cerebro spinal A. 1 case in 6th North Staffords. Cerebro Spinal Meningitis cases in the 5th North Staffords Regt. A circular developed & addressed from Cerebro-spinal fever in the honour review this correspondence. I am enclosing a weather report for the month showing the maximum & minimum temperature, the humidity of the air, the reading of the aneroid, the direction and force of the wind and the rainfall. W.H. Sydney Carter Lt. 17th Sanitary Section 46 Division	

46 Sanitary See MEDICAL Vol 2

WAR DIARY or INTELLIGENCE SUMMARY
Army Form C. 2118.

Place	Date	Hour	Summary of Events and Information	Remarks and references to Appendices
BAVINCOURT	1916 Sept 1		I have undertaken to disinfect all the dugouts and shelters in the trenches because of the number of lice. It is considered very probable that trench fever is caused by the bites of these & and I have been asked to destroy by disinfection all lice that may be left in the trenches when the troops are out of these dugouts and shelters. A party of 20 men were sent to me from the 2nd N.M. Field Ambulance. I put one of my N.C.O.s S/Sgt Moser in charge of them, they were billetted in BIENVILLERS where they started to disinfect all dugouts that could be reasonably made air tight, with formalin vapour, and all open shelters all dugouts which could not be made air tight, with formalin spray. A Mackenzie spray being used. I had to make the apparatus for creating the formalin vapour by putting a peacock flat tin containing 6 oz of Formalin on a lit Tripod with a jam tin containing 1½ pint of Methylated spirit under it for heating purposes. Then the Methylated spirit lasted 3½ of an hour	

WAR DIARY
or
INTELLIGENCE SUMMARY.
(Erase heading not required.)

Army Form C. 2118.

Place	Date	Hour	Summary of Events and Information	Remarks and references to Appendices
	Sept 14·15		the whole apparatus being placed in a 4 gall petrol tin surrounded by an inch of water. The dug-outs that could be made air-tight were closed up with paper and paste and disinfected with the above apparatus. The right sector occupied by the Leicester and Lincoln Infantry Brigade were treated first. Then these 20 men moved to BERLES and worked on the middle sector occupied by the 137th Infantry Brigade. When these were finished a fresh party of 20 men from the 1st N.M. Field Ambulance arrived and completed the disinfection in the North & Ratley Infantry Brigade. All the old bandages were taken out of these dug-outs and shelters and destroyed, also any old rubbish that might have been found there. I was sent to BOULOGNE and acted as M.O. to the 1st and 3rd Army Rest Camps	
	Sept 22		I visited and inspected the camp site of the 27th Reserve Park A.S.C. and made the following report and recommendations:— To ADMS 46th Division I visited today the site occupied by the 27th Reserve Park, No 3 Section found: (1) That the horse lines were in a very muddy condition (2) That the huts (five in number) have	

WAR DIARY
or
INTELLIGENCE SUMMARY.
(Erase heading not required.)

Army Form C. 2118.

Place	Date	Hour	Summary of Events and Information	Remarks and references to Appendices
	February 1917		At No 3 Camp, much praise is due to the O/C "B" Echelon of 46th Divisional D.A.C. for the excellent work that has been done in connection with the Sanitation of this camp. In the afternoon I visited the Baths at Warlincourt to see the alterations there. Arrangements are now complete for the separation of the Dirty from the Clean Clothing.	
	13–28th		To Gaudiempré — inspected several water carts belonging to some of the units of this Division at the stand-pipe at Gaudiempré. The others following upon the recent hard frost has played havoc with the fittings of some of the water-carts so I have decided to have all water carts in that Division systematically inspected by the NCO's of the Sanitary Section — with special reference to replacing of spare parts at present missing & having pumps put in working order. This to being done and a report will be submitted to A.D.M.S. in due course.	
	15th		Plans & Recommendations re Fly-proof Latrines sent through A.D.M.S. Office & "Q" Branch 46th Divl. Headquarters to CO.s of all units. Report re Measles cases sent to O/C Wrench Mission. — saw O/C No 8 Mobile Laboratory re Suspected Diphtheria cases amongst afternoon. There were no cases of "Chronic" Carriers arranged with O/C 58th *	
	17–19th		The civilians evacuated. — Preliminary arrangements for moving from this area. — Divisional Sanitary Section details with reference to "taking over".	

III.

Army Form C. 2118.

WAR DIARY
or
INTELLIGENCE SUMMARY.
(Erase heading not required.)

Place	Date	Hour	Summary of Events and Information	Remarks and references to Appendices
	Sept 6th		Metallic Poison Case applied to us by the Army Sanitary Committee. It forms the granulated zinc supplied for testing arsenic contained a small amount of arsenic which would prevent the test being very accurate for minute portions of this particular poison. I shall continue this class until all the Medical Officers have been notified. As present I am short of the necessary chemicals. These are being obtained from the Advanced Medical Stores. I visited the trenches occupied by the 5th Sherwood Foresters and inspected a latrine that had been erected by the M.O. after a pattern that he and I devised a few weeks previously. The main order being adopted by supports and expanded metal. Over this trench a wooden platform is placed so as to keep it fly and rat proof. An oil drum with top and bottom knocked out and a fly-proof vent on top and is placed in a hole in the platform. I attend a shelter covering the idea. When this latrine is used for excreta all the male urate and urine is first in to form a liquid mass. Then a sufficient quantity of cotton oil is deposited on the surface of the refuse mass and a fine film is formed turning it into a closed septic tank where anaerobic micro organisms can flourish. I am unable to express an opinion as to the working of this system until next month when it has had a fair	Appendix A

WAR DIARY
or
INTELLIGENCE SUMMARY.
(Erase heading not required.)

Army Form C. 2118.

Place	Date	Hour	Summary of Events and Information	Remarks and references to Appendices
	12th		troops & was chiefly used by them. The Camp Commandant was informed and the matter received immediate attention. The main source of water supply for St. Riquier & district is a Spring supply Map Ref. G.3.d.5.4. I inspected this spring along with an N.C.O. of this section & found it liable to surface pollution. The following report was accordingly prepared & sent to the A.D.M.S. 46th Division 11.xi.1916 I have to report that I have today inspected the Springs of a supply for Drinking Water at St. Riquier. Map Ref. G.3.d.5.4. The Water is of good quality (requires to scrub. Bk. Bond. Jar cart), the supply is abundant and the spring Basin is suitable for the filling of Water carts. Units from outlying districts are using these Springs as well as units stationed in St. Riquier. It is the best source of water supply in the Village. The roadway beside the stream abuts down towards the Springs with the result that the surface water from the roadway is contaminating the water. This has been especially noticeable since the recent heavy rains. I would recommend the erection of a concrete or brick wall 9" high & 10-12 ft. long on the embankment	11

WAR DIARY
or
INTELLIGENCE SUMMARY.
(Erase heading not required.)

Army Form C. 2118.

MEDICAL

Place	Date	Hour	Summary of Events and Information	Remarks and references to Appendices
St Riquier	1916. Nov 6th		Reported to the A.D.M.S., 46th Division for duty, the journey from the Headquarters of 2nd London Sanitary Coy, London, having taken nearly a week.	
	Nov. 6 – 9.		During this period I accompanied Capt N.W. Barbury on a tour of inspection of some of the Units in this Division. The information as to the disposition of the various Units & their general Sanitary situation, so kindly supplied by my Predecessor in office, has proved of inestimable value to me.	
			The Division arrived in the St Riquier Training Area upon November 2nd since which time no permanent sanitary appliances of any sort were found in any of the villages in this area. To help some of the Units to overcome their difficulties the Sanitary Section supplied 200 Oil Drums for Latrines and 150 Wash bowls (made from 4 gall. petrol tins) for ablution purposes. These Wash bowls were cut & fitted with wooden handles in the Sanitary Section workshops.	
	11th		The public urinal in Cathedral Square St Riquier was reported to be in an unsanitary state & was inspected. I found that the drain pipes and the surrounding ground had been soiled with human excreta. The Mayor, to whom the matter was referred, refused to take any action because the urinal had been put there by the British	

1.

WAR DIARY
or
INTELLIGENCE SUMMARY.
(*Erase heading not required.*)

Army Form C. 2118.

Instructions regarding War Diaries and Intelligence Summaries are contained in F.S. Regs., Part II. and the Staff Manual respectively. Title pages will be prepared in manuscript.

Hour, Date, Place	Summary of Events and Information	Remarks and references to Appendices
	Plan of Kitchen Table — after hammering flat solder seam 1/2 here. Tin showing join which must be hammered flat. ← 4' 0" → ← 1' 9" → Plan. Section.	

9

Army Form C. 2118.

46 D Cen¹

17 Sanitary Section

Vol 8

WAR DIARY
or
INTELLIGENCE SUMMARY.
(Erase heading not required.)

Place	Date	Hour	Summary of Events and Information	Remarks and references to Appendices
Hinn.	March 1917 1st		Divisional Headquarters (46th N. Midland) returned to Hinn from Gouy. The Sanitary Section rejoined its headquarters at Hinn and the sub-sections which had been left in this area under the 58th Division now came under my orders. The sub-section which had been detailed to accompany the 139th Infantry Brigade to the Ouis-st-Pierre Area now returned with that Brigade to the Hinn area.	
	5th		On my return from leave in England I reported to D.A.D.M.S. 46th Division.	
	6th		Inspected the Field Ambulance sites at Sauchinfer — discussed the question of the disposal of the baths & ablution effluent with Col. Hoskin — recommended the fitting of a filter bed and soakage pit & settling (related line to enable the effluent to be used again. Inspected the attractions recently made in ? M/A. The Incinerator + Drying Room in the same site & had the attached drawing prepared.	
	7th		As Major Vaughan D.A.D.M.S. has taken ill, I spent the forenoon helping Capt. J. Mullen A/DADMS with the routine office work.	
			Afternoon — to Rao — interviewed D.M.D.M.S. XVIII Corps re my Sergt. who is attached to him for Sanitary Inspector's duties in Rao. In the evening I paid the new ? St Amand & Scraupre. — Saw RE's re suggested Baths at	

1.

WAR DIARY or INTELLIGENCE SUMMARY

Army Form C. 2118.

MEDICAL

46 D Sanitary Sec.
Set 5

Place	Date	Hour	Summary of Events and Information	Remarks and references to Appendices
Puchevillers	1916. December 1st		In the morning I inoculated with T.A.B. eleven men of R.E. Divisional Signals. Preliminary arrangements were made with Divisional Gas Officer for the fitting of Small-Box respirators. Thereafter, accompanied by D.A.D.M.S. 46th Division, I inspected the huts at Puchevillers. The hutment suggestions re: improvements in this camp are now in the Appendix to last month's Diary. A further series of recommendations was now made to the Town Major. The work is proceeding satisfactorily under the direct supervision of a N.C.O. of this Sanitary Section.	A/A.
	Decr. 2-3.		Sans St Riquer & Riquichecourt visited. Here the same lack of permanent Sanitary appliances is in evidence throughout the whole area occupied by this Division in & around Puchevillers. There were practically no Sanitary appliances of a permanent nature. Fatigue parties from the various units have been busy clearing up collections of refuse from billetted districts & the units at St Riquer have installed incinerators. But permanent Latrines in the meantime, of course, are too to be adopted and so much valuable time is temporarily improved methods have to be resorted more difficult for the Sanitary squads. At last Sand the work is rendered more difficult for the Sanitary squads.	
	Decr. 3-4.		Inspected the N.C.Os & men under my command & found no cases of Scabies or other skin disease. A return has been made accordingly.	

WAR DIARY
or
INTELLIGENCE SUMMARY.

(Erase heading not required.)

Army Form C. 2118.

Place	Date	Hour	Summary of Events and Information	Remarks and references to Appendices
	11th–21st		above the Spring & the repair of the road leading to this important water supply. Much of the materials required could be obtained from an old Quarry situated about 100 yards from the Spring. Wellhi Kent O/c 17 San. Section. The matter was referred to the R.E. before we left the area, a pump had been installed and preliminary steps taken to remedy the nuisance. During the routine inspection of Cookers & Kitchens, I notice the lack of uniformity in kitchen administration; I have recommended that further copies of Appendix A. "Recommendations for all Kitchens & Cookhouses of the Division" be prepared & issued to the units concerned. This is being done.	
	22nd		A case of Dysentery (suspected) was reported as having occurred in the 138th Brigade Machine Gun Coy at Wef Moulin. Inspected the village & found conditions there unsatisfactory from a Sanitary point of view. It was deemed advisable to attach an N.C.O. from this section to the Machine Gun Coy to supervise Sanitary improvements there in accordance with R.A.M.C. Circular Memo. 56.	

III.

Army Form C. 2118.

WAR DIARY
or
INTELLIGENCE SUMMARY.
(Erase heading not required.)

Place	Date	Hour	Summary of Events and Information	Remarks and references to Appendices
Henin	1917 March 8th (contd)		St Amand camp site. I made suggestions & recommendations to R.E.'s re: disposal of the soapy water. These will be put into effect if its work at the Baths is to proceed. Inspected Camp site at St Amand. Latrines still unsatisfactory. Arrangements have been made to have pegs, trench plug but, at present, it seems impossible to obtain materials and labour for the making of the box fly-proof seats.	
	9th		I saw the Town Major there with reference to an accumulation of tins at the incinerator site in the Valley Camp. - advised that these be neatly stacked and left until transport is obtained for their removal. - on to Foncquevillers - saw Town Major & actg. Staff Captain of 139th Infantry Brigade re: Water supply for troops in the forward area.	
			Water supply report sent in. Foncquevillers & Souastre was forwarded to A.D.M.S. 46th Division. An amended report was sent to D.D.M.S. V Corps. when 1/DADMS 46th Dn.	Appendix B & C.
	10th		I saw Capt. Evans of Headquarters 46th Divl. R.A. in consultation with 1/DADMS 46th Div. re: German trenches. The necessary precautions were taken by me - Isolation Diagram, Disinfection & Examination of Contacts and a report was duly submitted to ADMS 46th Dn.	
	11-12th		Inspection of Billets & Hutts at Gaudiempre, St Amand, Sombrin & D.26 Central.	

WAR DIARY
or
INTELLIGENCE SUMMARY.
(Erase heading not required.)

Army Form C. 2118.

Place	Date	Hour	Summary of Events and Information	Remarks and references to Appendices
			no floor boards and were situated at a lower level than the horse lines & was informed during heavy rainfall the storm water off the horse lines flows down to and through the huts. I think this is quite possible judging from the lie of the field. The M.O. informs me that there is an abnormal amount of sickness which in his opinion is due to the unhealthiness of the camp site. I am of opinion that the camp site is unhealthy and is not in a fit state to be occupied during the coming Autumn and Winter months. I recommend:- (1) That the units occupying this site should vacate it as soon as possible (2) That a fresh billet be allotted to them. W.K. Pashmy Capt O/c Divisional Sanitary Section 46th Division	
	22/9/16		My report was forwarded to H.Q by the A.D.M.S and the unit was removed to another and better site. I took a class of our medical officers and instructed them in the use of the	
Sept 24				

WAR DIARY
or
INTELLIGENCE SUMMARY.

Army Form C. 2118.

Place	Date	Hour	Summary of Events and Information	Remarks and references to Appendices
	Dec 25th		Adjut. Infd. & sent to A.D.M.S. re the Baths throughout the Divisional area.	
	Dec 26th		Inspected camp site at St Amand. The work proceeds slowly now because of the scarcity of timber.	
	Dec 27th		To Wallincourt, Grincourt & Gonzeaucourt & also to 2nd N.M. Field Ambulance at Gonzeaucourt to inspect the various sanitary arrangements.	
	Dec 28th		At Valley Camp Sericourt. To try to hasten on the work of building the new latrines. The shortage of timber is proving a great draw-back.	
	Dec 29-31		Routine Inspection of camps etc. Much constructional work is in progress. Infectious Diseases:- Total number during the month under review – 13. Measles 1. – 137th Brigade Machine Gun Coy. Scarlet Fever 1. – 5/18 How Batty. att. 247th (W.R.) Bde R.F.A. Diphtheria 5. – 5th N. Staffs 2 cases; 6 N. Staffs, 8th Notts & Derbys & North Irish Horse 1 case each. Dysentery 3. (suspected) - 2nd N.M. Field Amb., 4th Lincolns Regt, & 4th Notts & Derbys, 1 case each. Cerebro-spinal meningitis 1 case in 5th Lincolns. Tuberculosis (lungs) 2 cases: 138 Mac. Gun Coy & 4th Lincolns, one case each.	

VIII.

WAR DIARY
or
INTELLIGENCE SUMMARY.
(Erase heading not required.)

Army Form C. 2118.

Place	Date	Hour	Summary of Events and Information	Remarks and references to Appendices
	Decr. 15.		During my inspection of the area I found that many of the permanent latrines were fitted with biscuit tins as buckets, in such a way as to separate the urine from the faeces. I find that this is quite unsatisfactory because the tins leak & after a few days and the ground becomes very foul. Oil-chunam & latrine buckets are being used to replace the tins as quickly as possible. Sample of water from Well No. 7 at Inghinville — heavy sediment; animal matter. No installed Vision detected. Bacteriological test done — Milky lactose-fermenting organisms present after 24 hrs. on lactose Agar. The well thus remains "Antityphoid" & "plaguous" & the windlass rope & bucket have been removed. In the afternoon I inspected the Divisional Laundry at Pas & found the general arrangements satisfactory & the latrines & the incinerator in a clean & satisfactory condition.	
	Decr. 16.		Attended Sanitary Conference & Demonstration of Sanitary Appliances at St Pol with DADMS 46th Division. I was pleased to note that quite a number of the demonstration have been sent by the 46th Divisional models exhibited at the demonstration (Sanitary Section). Took with me the two models of urinals illustrated in the Sanitary Section. After this we made from a Lucent tin was the work of a Sanitary fatigue man of the 1/5 N. Staffordshire Regt.	Off. C.

Army Form C. 2118.

WAR DIARY
or
INTELLIGENCE SUMMARY.
(Erase heading not required.)

Instructions regarding War Diaries and Intelligence Summaries are contained in F.S. Regs., Part II and the Staff Manual respectively. Title pages will be prepared in manuscript.

Place	Date	Hour	Summary of Events and Information	Remarks and references to Appendices
Hinn.	1917 March 22nd–24th		During this period, units of 46th Division moved from this area. The Town Major at Henin left one man to clean off the public sites, however by visiting arm light duty men which were attached to me for Sanitary work I have managed to have this site cleaned up.	
	25th		Camp site occupied by A Echelon 46th D.A.C. inspected along with Capt Wood. R.A.M.C. the Medical Officer of the unit.	
	26th–30th		Routine Inspections of Camp sites, Billets &c left by 46th Divisional Troops. Arrangements made to station a N.C.O. of this Section for Water duties in the forward area.	
	31st		Rode today to the villages in the forward area, visiting Tonquilles, Gomiecourt, Ervart, Ayette & Mayenville. Desolation everywhere. No wells discovered – very few troops in this area now – am having a thorough inspection of the area made for the presence of Wells &c. A report will be ready for next month's Diary. I do not propose to include in this Diary a report of Infectious Cases because the 46th Division did not occupy this area during the whole month, many cases that were brought to my notice really referred to other areas. Attended a Meteorological Class F.	App. F.

Nicolas Gebbie
Capt. R.A.M.C.T.
o/c No 17 Sanitary Section.

V.

WAR DIARY
or
INTELLIGENCE SUMMARY.
(Erase heading not required.)

Army Form C. 2118.

Place	Date	Hour	Summary of Events and Information	Remarks and references to Appendices
Henu	1917 March 13th		Today I received instructions from A.D.M.S. 46th Division to take over the command of the Divisional Laundry during the temporary absence of Capt. S.R.C. Harman R.A.M.C. Collection & distribution of clothing is at present being done at Henu. Washing is being done at the 137th Infantry Brigade Laundry at Pommier and at V Corps Laundry at Amplier. N.C.O's & men of 14th Sanitary Section to be held in readiness as reserve Stretcher-bearers for work at Advanced Dressing Station, Fonquevillers, if required.	
	14th "		Afternoon went to D.D.M.S.' Conference at V Corps Headquarters, Achieux. Made arrangements for the treatment of soiled Burice Dress — is drying, brushing and viming — by Laundry Staff at No 8 Billet, Henu.	
	15th "		Afternoon to Gaudiempre in consultation with Col. Hodder o/c 1/3 N.M. Field Ambulance, re treatment of contacts of a Measles case at the Field Ambulance. To 43 CCS to see Major Maughan D.A.D.M.S. 46th Div. Eight duty men attached this section start work on a Brick incinerator at Henu under the supervision of R.Qr Master of this section. Inspected the latrine sites (public) at Henu.	
	16th "		Evening; Assisted A.D.M.S. & D.A.D.M.S. 46th Division at a medical board on Laundry Staff. The men passed "fit" will work on the latrine carts at Pommiercourt.	

111.

WAR DIARY or INTELLIGENCE SUMMARY

Army Form C. 2118.

Place	Date	Hour	Summary of Events and Information	Remarks and references to Appendices
			Infectious Diseases (continued). Two cases of Diphtheria occurred amongst the civilians in this area during the month of December 1916, were notified to me & the necessary precautions were taken. 1) Child 8 yrs. at 105 Rue de Barleu commence died from Diphtheria on 11.xii.16. 7 civilian contacts received a prophylactic dose of Anti-diphtheria serum. 9 8 soldiers of 6th S. Staffords also injected with Anti-diphtheritic serum. & Billet & Baln & room used by child were all disinfected. 2) Child at Rue St Amand Suaste no 120 notified Diphtheria - onset 10.xii.16. I saw this case in consultation with Capt. Stell R.M.O. 17th Warwicks, the diagnosis verified the House has been disinfected. but the swab taken proved negative. Sporadic cases of Diphtheria keep occurring in the village close to the div. This has been going on for some months now, so after consultation with O/C No 8 Mobile Laboratory, I determined to have swabs taken from all civilians in Somastre in the hope of discovering a possible source of this infection. Over 200 from a total so far with the help of Capt. Stell, to have taken. The investigation is being continued. Of 1518 civilians still negative results. I am enclosing a copy of the Meteorological report for the month. W. Webbie, Capt. R.A.M.C.(T). o/c 14 Sanitary Section, 46 Division.	

WAR DIARY
or
INTELLIGENCE SUMMARY.
(Erase heading not required.)

Army Form C. 2118.

Place	Date	Hour	Summary of Events and Information	Remarks and references to Appendices
			trial. I have also asked this M.O. to institute another scheme for disposal of excreta in the trenches. It is only to be carried out when the latrine bucket system is in vogue. My idea is to have a trench leading from each latrine which will open out into a trench 6 ft wide and 13 ft long. The excreta from the buckets will be buried in shallow trenches 2 ft x 1 ft by 1 ft deep. There will be sufficient for about 26 days. In each case the excreta is covered with surface loam soil which will contain sufficient nitrogenous producing bacteria. I think by the time the last hole is used, the first hole will have completely consumed the excreta placed in it. The M.O. for this unit - 5th Sherwood Foresters has promised to carry out this scheme for me as soon as he can and I hope to report on it next month. During the month ending today there have been 42 cases of Infectious Disease <u>Diphtheria 25 Cases</u> The following is a list giving the units in which Diphtheria occurred: 4th Lincolns - 7 8 Sherwood Foresters - 5 5th Lincolns - 3 5th Leicesters - 3 1/1 N.M. R.E. Field Co. - 2 6 North Staffords - 1 5 North Staffords - 3	Appendix B
Sept 30				

Army Form C. 2118.

WAR DIARY
or
INTELLIGENCE SUMMARY.
(Erase heading not required.)

Place	Date	Hour	Summary of Events and Information	Remarks and references to Appendices
			Measles: 3 cases occurred in 5th N. Staffs Regt. B Coy, 6 Platoon. The 4th contacts were strictly isolated for 16 days & their billet was disinfected every fourth day.	
			Scarlet Fever: 2 Paras + "Cicioths 1 & 6th N. Staffs 1.	
			Diphtheria: 12 cases + "Cicioths 4 cases & 1 "carrier"; 4th Cicioths 2 cases; 1st Monmouths 2 cases; 5th Ricciotes, 2nd N.M. Fld Amb. & 1/2 N.M. Fld. Coy RE 1 case each.	
			As mentioned in Diary for last month, the search for "Carriers" + "Cicioths was continued. The contacts of the carrier are mentioned above have received a prophylactic injection of Anti-Diphtheritic Serum.	
			Enteric Group:	
			Typhoid Fever 1 case; In 8th N. Staffs 2 cases; Irvirl Signal Boy, 2nd N.M. Fld Amb, 230th Brigade R.F.A. & 4th Notts & Derby Regt. one case each.	
			Enteric Group: 2 cases; 6th S. Staffs & 231st Bgde. R.F.A. one case each.	
			Paratyphoid A: 3 cases; 5th N. Staffs 2 cases & 6th N. Staffs 1 case.	
			Paratyphoid B: 5 cases; 1st Monmouths, 137th Bgde. Mac Gun Coy & 5th N. Staffs one case each.	
			All the contacts of the Enteric Group cases have been inoculated with mixed T.A.B. Vaccine.	
			V.	

Army Form C. 2118.

46 D Sanitary
Vol 6

WAR DIARY
or
INTELLIGENCE SUMMARY.
(Erase heading not required.)

Place	Date	Hour	Summary of Events and Information	Remarks and references to Appendices
Aine.	February 1919			
	1.	1.	Inspected Sanitary Appliances at the Baths & Laundry at Pas; thereafter inspected No. 2 Camp Pas Abbs along with the Town Major; arranged for contacts of cases of Ambro-spiral fever the inspected evacuated to O.C. U.S. Mobile Laboratory & made preliminary arrangements for disinfection of the hut.	
	2.		Arranged for treatment & c. of certain whale scab amongst the civilians at Aine. To Corignaux to inspect the stand-pipe from which certain water outs of this Division receive their water-supplies — then to Corignaux Rest Camp & inspected 5th & 7th Notts & Derby transport lines. Arrangements made to have any old accumulations of rubbish behind the Fatchen buried as soon as thaw sets in. The trench system has been started here, and, as soon as thaw is established, will be further extended.	
	3.		A fresh case of Mumps at Billet & Aine notified, visited & treated. Members of 58th Divisional Sanitary Section were detailed for duty in the various villages throughout the area. Inspected 139th Brigade School in Pas Valley at Aine with D.A.A. & Q.M.G. 46th Divn. Corignaux Rest Camp which would afford to be in 5th Army Area etc is occupied by 46th Divisional troops. Arranged that the sanitary condition be reported on by me as previously — sent in report re unburied dead horse at D.26 Central.	
	4.		To Corim to see Lt/Col 36th Sanitary Section re)	

1.

WAR DIARY
or
INTELLIGENCE SUMMARY.
(Erase heading not required.)

Army Form C. 2118.

Place	Date	Hour	Summary of Events and Information	Remarks and references to Appendices

1st Monmouths - 1   1st N.M. Field Ambulance - 1   R.E. Signals - 1
232nd Bde. R.F.A. - 1

In the ft. of 4th Lincolns there have been found 13 Carrier Cases - These have been sent to the 1/3 N.M. Field Ambulance where they are detained until their throats show 3 negative swabs at the interval of 48 hours each. Swabbing the 8th Sherwood Foresters are being examined now and so far 2 carrier cases have been found. The billets of all cases have been disinfected and the contacts of acute cases have either been inoculated or isolated for 10 days.

Dysentery - 4 Cases of Bacillary.
The following is a list of cases showing units:-

5th Lincolns - 2   1st Monmouths - 1   5th So. Staffords - 1
8th Sherwood Foresters (attached to H.Q. 138 Bde.) - 1   2/1 N.M. R.E. Field Co. - 1
Mobile Veterinary Section - 1

The last two cases (2/1 N.M. R.E. and Mobile Vet Section) have been traced to an estaminet in L'ARBRET where one child died of dysentery and another was ill with it.

6

WAR DIARY
or
INTELLIGENCE SUMMARY.

Army Form C. 2118.

Place	Date	Hour	Summary of Events and Information	Remarks and references to Appendices
Héni	February 1917 20th		Divisional Headquarters moved to Gouy-en-Artois & this Sanitary Section was moved. The arrangements were made whereby two Subsections, each consisting of a Sergt. and three O.Rs, were left with the two Infantry Brigades although finally the administration of the 58th Divisional Sanitary Section. I found that there were practically no permanent Sanitary Appliances in Gouy. The plans of a Sanitation scheme for the village were in the Town Major's hands but difficulty had been experienced by him in obtaining materials & labour. Temporary measures were adopted but little of a permanent nature was accomplished as the Divisional Headquarters was recalled to Hénu upon 1.III.17.	
Gouy.			Infectious Diseases: During the month under review there have been 43 cases of infectious diseases amongst units in this area. Of these, there were — 13 Diphtheria: — (10 Positive & 2 suspected). 23 Measles: — (14 German & 4 suspected German & 5 English). 5 Mumps: — (3 Positive & 2 suspected). 1. Cerebro-Spinal Meningitis. 2. Tuberculosis (Lungs). The units concerned were widely scattered, but in 15th Leicesters there were 5 cases & typho were taken to have the contacts isolated. Only one other case occurred. IV.	

Army Form C. 2118.

WAR DIARY
or
INTELLIGENCE SUMMARY.
(Erase heading not required.)

Place	Date	Hour	Summary of Events and Information	Remarks and references to Appendices
Elisa.	March 1917 17th		To Harlincourt & Guincourt – inspected 46th Divisional A.S.C. Headquarters, Billets, Sanitary arrangements & horse-lines. Much old manure has been left round the horse lines. I find, on enquiry, that the ASC remove the fresh manure each day to the dump and that, when transport is available, the old manure is removed also. I recommended to the Town Major the establishment of deep trench latrines with fly-proof seats to replace the existing bucket system. Sites chosen along with Lt/Cpl T.C. Brown of this section.	
	18th – 20th		It was decided to establish advanced Divl. Headquarters at Chateau de la Haie. Visited the site each day and chose sites for latrines, urinals, incinerators &c. Tranquillere, Gommecourt & Ecoust also visited with a view to ascertaining possible sources of water supply. All wells in Gommecourt & Ecoust have been recently chlorinated. An interesting German Bath was discovered in a cellar in Gommecourt - for description and drawing of the same by L/Cpl Ashkam of this section see Appendix D to this Diary.	App. D & E.
	21st		Noted that Sanitary Returns attached to Infantry Divisions are now Army troops & are under the direct supervision of Corps. In the evening I attended a Sanitary Conference at the office of DDMS V Corps.	IV.

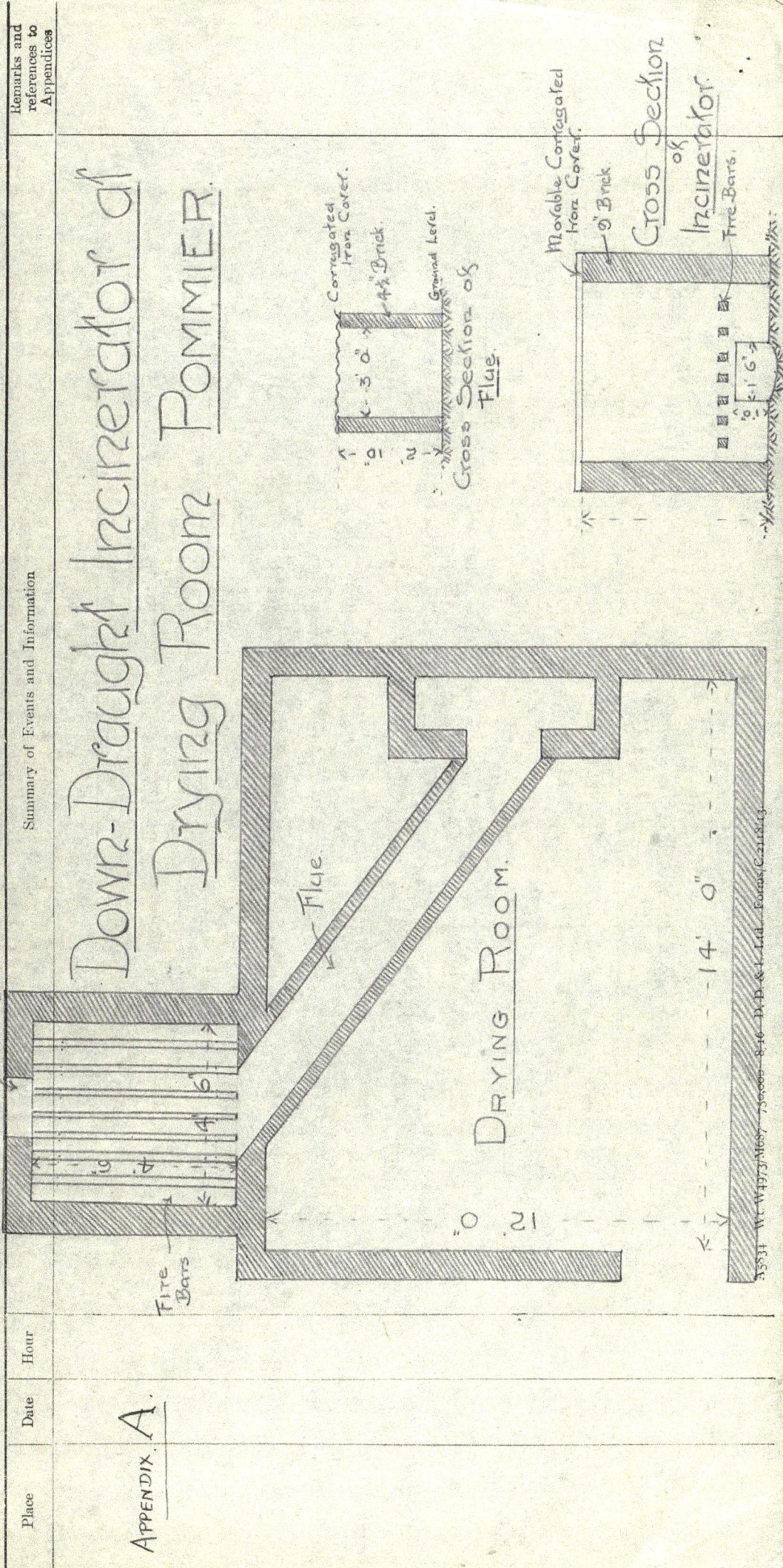

WAR DIARY
or
INTELLIGENCE SUMMARY.
(Erase heading not required.)

Army Form C. 2118.

Place	Date	Hour	Summary of Events and Information	Remarks and references to Appendices
			5 No. Staffs. - 1 48th Heavy Artillery Group - 1 4th Entrenching Battalion - 1 These cases were isolated so far as their billets were concerned and were daily examined by the M.O., their morning temperatures being specially recorded. All the billets were disinfected. Mumps - 1 Case 11th N.M. Field Ambulance The billet in this case was disinfected. Enteric Group - 1 Case 5th No. Staffords All contacts were inoculated with mixed vaccine and the billet disinfected. Paratyphoid A - 1 Case 5 No. Staffords. This officer has rejoined his unit one hour before reporting ill. He had been away from his unit for 6 weeks.	

WAR DIARY
or
INTELLIGENCE SUMMARY.

Army Form C. 2118.

Place	Date	Hour	Summary of Events and Information	Remarks and references to Appendices
	23rd		Lt. Rlynis arrived at Frohen le Grand. Two Sanitary N.C.O.s were sent on in advance to Puchvin to assist the Town Major 1) for Water/Butties 2) for general sanitation.	
	25th		He arrived in the Puchvin area & found very few permanent Sanitary appliances. Some of the billets in the outlying in latter's area have been left in a very dirty state. These are being cleaned.	
	28th		Visits at Puchvin inspected & short & recommendations sent to the Town Major. A fatigue party under the supervision of an N.C.O. of this section. Pro confirmed with by the Sanitation of those Pits & I hope in next months Diary to be able to give a detailed account of the work done.	
			During the month under review, 39 cases of Infectious Disease were notified & investigated. Myalgia 3 cases. Scarlet fever 2 ". Diphtheria 12 ". Enteric Group 14 ". (suspected) Dysentery 5 ". Pneumonia 3 ".	IV.

Place	Date	Hour	Summary of Events and Information	Remarks and references to Appendices
	December 6th – 14th		During this period, I made myself acquainted with the general Sanitary arrangements of the present area. Both by personal inspection & from reports by my N.C.O.s. A routine inspection of the Baths throughout the area was commenced & a report & sketch plans of the various baths were sent to A.D.M.S. 46th Division for VII Corps upon 24th December 1916. At St Amand, I visited the site of the arrangements with the Capt of the Divisional School for the instruction of Sanitary appliances for the use of those attending the School course. The R.E. had the work done & the Sanitary Section supplied Latrine trails, wash-bowls. The arrangements were completed four days before the School opened. My attention was drawn to the question of establishing a drying room at Pommier near the Baths. I interviewed the Staff Captain of 137th Brigade & discussed details as to construction, requirements &c. An incinerator (brick) has been built & its flue taken through the drying room & up the existing chimney. This work is practically completed & I trust it shall be able to give plans & record success in next months Diary. I have drawn the attention of the Town Major to an accumulation of rubbish at Billet 90, on the ditch alongside & in the camp-site at St Amand. The two former have been cleared up & the latter is being dealt with now.	

IV.

	Army Form C. 2118.
WAR DIARY *or* **INTELLIGENCE SUMMARY.** (Erase heading not required.)	

Place	Date	Hour	Summary of Events and Information	Remarks and references to Appendices
	January 1917 4th		Visited Horse Watering Station ; & on my return, arranged for the Section NCOs at present attached to that Stations & others to slaughter out. This was considered desirable because the NCOs in Fonquevillers & Bienvillers were showing a tendency to develop minor ailments eg Influenza &c and were showing signs of mental fatigue as well. The Section Lifts are temporarily posted to the Sound Majors (at the main villages until the Sections are more complete. The results of this change have fully justified the action taken.	
	5th		Visited the 1st, 2nd, & 3rd Field Ambulances today with Major Warham DADMS. Found the sanitary arrangements generally satisfactory.	
	6-8th		Inspection of sites at Gaudiempré, Walincourt & Gincourt with Town Majors also to Souastre in S6 with DADMS 46th Division to inspect the Valley Camp. The new latrines are now being erected.	
	9th		Y. Souastre & on to Fonquevillers - saw Town Major with reference to the store of water (Browne can(ily)) in Fonquevillers - am endeavouring to replace its leaking A-Gallon Tins with 2 gall. petrol tins efficiently stoppered &soon as possible, & to have the water stored in that this changed more frequently. - visited Advanced Dressing Station at Fonquevillers & arranged to found up Chimns spouts for the Latrine tents. Baths not visited as hay settling had commenced.	

WAR DIARY or INTELLIGENCE SUMMARY.

Army Form C. 2118.

(Erase heading not required.)

Place	Date 1917	Hour	Summary of Events and Information	Remarks and references to Appendices
	January 22nd		To Sanitary Conference, III rd Army at H.Q. with Major Maugham DADMS 46th Division & Major O'Reilly DADMS XVIII Corps.	Appendix E & F.
	23rd – 31st		Investigation f/Mumps Outbreak amongst the school children of Albert. will refer to ADMS & to O/c French Mission 46th Division in the Difficulty.	G.
	26th		Inspected Sanitary arrangements of 6th N. Staffs Regt. at [?] Amend with DADMS 46th Div. with reference to the building of a new incinerator on the 1st N.M. Field Ambulance to define Col. Ibrothie's with reference to the building of a new incinerator on the 1st N.M. Field Ambulance site.	
	27th		Inspected Sanitary arrangements of 46th Divisional Train.	
	28th		To Sonastre – re Baths. – Pipes have been frozen – matter referred to R.E.	
	29th		To Gaudiempre & 2nd N.M. Field Ambulance.	
	30th		To see new John Major at Sonastre.	
	31st		Inspected C.232 R.F.A. (Horse Lines, cookhouse &c), 141st Cog. Corps R.E. huts, cookhouse &c & the Public Urinals & Latrines at Gaudiempre. This arrangement f/Public Urinals Horse tanks which have been emptied periodically in the case of the urinal when the cess pools (to alter them) yet return that present artel this matter will receive due consideration.	

VI

WAR DIARY
or
INTELLIGENCE SUMMARY.

Army Form C. 2118.

Place	Date	Hour	Summary of Events and Information	Remarks and references to Appendices
	Dec. 17th		Today, five light-duty men were sent by A.D.M.S. 46th Division to be attached to the Sanitary Section for duty in the workshops. Without the help of these men it would have been impossible to meet the demands for Sanitary appliances from the various units in the trenches. I inspected the Baths at Gaudiempre along with Town Major and an officer of R.E. The shortage of fuel is keenly felt at these baths so I have suggested that an incinerator be built close to the baths fitted with a water tank, this tank to be connected with the washing tank at the baths. A certain amount of economy in fuel would thus be effected.	
	Dec. 18th		Today I made a careful inspection of the Latrines at Sovastre [Souastre] and that with the exception of the Valley Camp, the latrines are well distributed over the various areas of the village & are adequate for the numbers of troops in the village. A report & suggestions for a new system of Latrines for the Valley Camp at Sovastre has been sent to the Town Major & the work is now in progress.	
	December 18-31.		I am having the throats of all civilians in Sovastre swabbed in a search for Diphtherial Carriers. — Full particulars of this investigation are to be found in this diary under the heading "Infectious Diseases."	
	Dec. 19.		I inspected A.S.C. Supply Column at Glmas [Gomas?] found the Sanitary arrangements fairly satisfactory.	

VI.

WAR DIARY or INTELLIGENCE SUMMARY

Army Form C. 2118.

Place	Date	Hour	Summary of Events and Information	Remarks and references to Appendices
London	1917			
	2nd	5. — 11.	Medically inspected the sick at 138th Brigade Depôt, St. Amand. Afternoon to a conference at office of D.D.M.S. 18th Corps.	
	3rd		Sanitary officer & personnel of 58th Divisional Sanitary Section attached to this Sanitary Section for instruction. During this period the various members of the 58th Divisional Sanitary Section were shown the various Sanitary Appliances throughout the area and special attention was paid to the system of trench sanitation in vogue in this area. The various camps were also visited and the methods of dealing with various difficulties discussed.	
	12th		Inspected Lines occupied by Heavy (Corps) Artillery at Henu. — saw Staff-Captain re accumulation of rubbish which requires removing. Deep trench latrines are being put in. — Inspected 139th Brigade Depôt Camp at Couaste. Fly-Trap latrines is in course of construction there.	
			111th Army Pattern fly trap latrines made at the Sanitary Section Workshop has been installed at Henu. It is working satisfactorily. A new camp (No. 4) is being occupied at Henu.	
	13th		Inspected the various camps at Pas Huts. Some of 58th Divn. R.E.'s are at work on new latrines. The incinerator by South Irish Horse Sat. No 2 Camp, some of 58th Divn. R.E.'s attended to. Town Major asked to see to this sites are not satisfactory	

for a month. In all these units all contacts are examined daily for 16 days. One of my N.C.O.s is posted to the unit to report and advise on the sanitation. All cases of diarrhoea are carefully watched and any suspicious cases sent to Field Ambulance.

Scarlet Fever - 4 Cases

The following is a list of cases showing units :-

230 Bde R.F.A. - 1   5th Lincolns - 1   1st Monmouths - 1
4th Entrenching Battalion - 1

This disease was introduced into this Division by some reinforcements which came up in August. The above 4 cases may be considered sporadic ones. I have arranged to have all contacts rigidly isolated and billets disinfected.

German Measles - 3 Cases

The following is a list of cases showing units

WAR DIARY
or
INTELLIGENCE SUMMARY.
(Erase heading not required.)

Army Form C. 2118.

Place	Date	Hour	Summary of Events and Information	Remarks and references to Appendices
	1917			
	January 3rd		Inspected the various Incinerator sites at Flinu. All satisfactory except that in CR road. Two old pit incinerators with chimneys have broken down almost completely – probably due to the recent heavy rains – and some difficulty is being experienced in dealing with the feces. Plans were drawn up, materials have been obtained & skilled labour promised for the construction of a new type synche brick incinerator on this site. The first trenches the end of the month the trenches the work being proceeded with but a start will be made with the R.E. of 3rd Pioneer Batln. R.E.'s tomorrow as twenty 46th Divisional Ammunition Column along with the Divisional Inspected the construction of two corrugated iron incinerators to medical officer. suggested from the camp-site. This has been done & is satisfactory. died with the subsoil from the camp-site. This has been done & is satisfactory. The horse lines are being rapidly improved & rendered weather-proof. the manure is being carted away daily to the stores Dumps.	
	afternoon		To Flomard to discuss or "preventable diseases or army horses" by A.D.V.S. 46th Division.	
	4th		Inspected Sanitary arrangements at 139th Infantry Brigade Bombing School near Flinu. Latrines are being improved. Water-supply is by water-cart from Origicourt to tanks near the school – thence to the huts [?] in petrol-tins. The water in the cart was efficiently chlorinated.	

11.

WAR DIARY
or
INTELLIGENCE SUMMARY.
(Erase heading not required.)

Army Form C. 2118.

Place	Date	Hour	Summary of Events and Information	Remarks and references to Appendices
	Decr. 20th		Am having two corrugated iron incinerators built for temporary use at the valley camp at Obrasth to help to get rid of an outstanding accumulation of rubbish implicated the baths at the Camp. The pump for supplying water to the baths is out of order, but the matter has been referred to R.E.[?]	
	Decr. 21st		At St Amand, the latrine & incinerator site is very bad — to be closed as soon as possible. A new site more suitable one, has been chosen, & as soon as the material come to hand, a new permanent latrine will be built there & a new & bigger brick incinerator. On to Berneville — managed to inspect the two sets of baths there in the intervals between shelling. The tanks at this baths are not protected sufficiently from shrapnel. Investigated a Cuebro-Guinel fever case at D.D.Amkd & arranged for the necessary precautions to be taken.	Appendix. D.
	Decr. 22nd		I was sent by A.D.M.S. 46th Division to investigate a complaint re condition of billet 34 Rucheur recently vacated by 46th Division & now occupied by 40th Division C.R.A.	Appendix E.
	Decr. 24th		Report sent to A.D.M.S. re accumulation of rubbish behind chateau at Hanne, for some time used as Officers mess kitchen 40th Division C.R.A. VII.	

WAR DIARY
OR
INTELLIGENCE SUMMARY.
(Erase heading not required.)

Army Form C. 2118.

Place	Date	Hour	Summary of Events and Information	Remarks and references to Appendices
	January 1917	12th	Saw three cases of Measles amongst Civilian children at Henu in consultation with Capt Sharpe actg. R.M.O. 2nd D.A.C. Have arranged that the necessary precautions & have offered suggestions as to treatment & these have been adopted.	
		13th	In the afternoon visited the incinerator site at Henu with the D.A.D.M.S. 46th Div.	
		14-19th	During this week I have had attached the O/C Sanitary Section 59th Division. He had been sent over from England to have a week's practical instruction in the work of a Sanitary Section at the front. During the week I endeavoured to make Capt. White a/c 59th San. Sctn. acquainted with the working of the Section, with the general Sanitary Arrangements & with the special problems at present receiving my attention.	
		17th	Visit from D.A.D.M.S. (Sanitation) 1st Army. To the Anti Vd. Gas Huts inspected 231st Bgde R.F.A. & to Valley Camp, Souastre.	
		18th	With Capt White to Pommier, Bienvillers & the left sector of our trenches. Inspected the general sanitary arrangements there along with the R.M.O 5th N. Staffs — made out its enquiry into the methods of Manure Disposal by the various	Appendix D
		19-21st	Made arrangements for an enquiry into the methods of Manure Disposal by the various Divisional Units — a sketch map of manure dumps in the area was prepared.	

Army Form C. 2118.

WAR DIARY
or
INTELLIGENCE SUMMARY.
(Erase heading not required.)

Instructions regarding War Diaries and Intelligence Summaries are contained in F.S. Regs., Part II. and the Staff Manual respectively. Title pages will be prepared in manuscript.

Place	Date	Hour	Summary of Events and Information	Remarks and references to Appendices
			Dysentery (Suspected) 5 cases, 138th Bgde Mac. Gun Coy 2 cases, 5th Lincolns, 6th N. Staffs & 5th N. Staffs one case each. Pneumonia; 3 cases. 137th Bgde Head Quarters, 4th Lincolns & Divl Supply column one case each.	
			I enclose a copy of the Weather report for the month shewing Barometric Pressure (an aneroid) Max & Min. Temperatures, Humidity of the Air, Direction & force of the Wind & the Rainfall.	Appendix C.
			W. Gibbs. Lieut R.A.M.C.(T). O/c 14th th Sanitary Section. 46th Division.	

WAR DIARY
or
INTELLIGENCE SUMMARY.
(Erase heading not required.)

Army Form C. 2118.

17 Sanitary Sec: 40/10
9th Div 6

Place	Date	Hour	Summary of Events and Information	Remarks and references to Appendices
Henu	January 1917 1st		The Sanitary Section fitted up suitable temporary latrines & Urinals for the children of three at Divisional Headquarters, which the chateau where a Nurse Du was held for staff children in its wing.	
	2nd		St Amand V — inspected the Camp site there with Medical Officer 6th O.B. Staffs Regt. Fatigue parties are busy clearing up the old incinerator site — there is an extensive accumulation of old hut rubbish still & a latrine for this camp is practically at a stand-still owing to the work on the new latrine for Sanlan	
			An Ste Bonnieul — inspected Baths, Laundry & Drying Room also three latrine. The two incinerators built along with the Jones and/or "Alsgnes" brick incinerator has been erected behind the Drying Room and by adopting the downward draught principle, the flue has been tried to fans but at the floor level, is carried through the drying room and up the existing brick chimney. Difficulties were experienced at first with the draught but the incinerator has very forward & are cross bricks on the chimney-top removed with excellent results. The incinerator has proved most useful in dealing with the refuse from the village. As no soap-trap exists for the bath effluent, I handpicked trench m" made at the Sanitary Section workshop. The Section has also supplied two T-winds (drawings of same in Post-months' Diary Appendix) for the winch over the baths. The peep-box was made by the Sanitary Section carpenter, has been installed and is working satisfactorily 26.7.17	Appendix A.

WAR DIARY
or
INTELLIGENCE SUMMARY.
(Erase heading not required.)

Army Form C. 2118.

Place	Date	Hour	Summary of Events and Information	Remarks and references to Appendices
	Dec. 4th		To Hesru to make preliminary arrangements for "Taking over" from 49th Divisional Sanitary Section – In the absence of the Sanitary Officer of that Division, the D.A.D.M.S. 49th Division very kindly handed over the maps & plans of the area & showed me a few of the places requiring urgent attention.	
	Dec. 5th		Sent on in advance my Sanitary Section Sergt. to take over from 49th Divisional N.C.O.'s at Hesru, St Amand, Ourastre, Gauchinpre, Halvincourt, Bermerie, Bienvillers & Hongeuillers. The camp out at Hendures was again inspected & the work is still proceeding fairly satisfactorily however the Town Majors Depts some difficulty in obtaining a fatigue party as the various units are preparing to move out of the area. Arrangements made for billets in all these Brigade areas recently occupied by public cars to be disinfected as soon as they were empty. This disinfection was carried out by N.C.O.'s from this Sanitary Section.	
	Dec. 6th		By arrangement with 29th Div. the two motor lorries conveyed the stores of the Sections from Arvillers to Hesru & return. Two journeys were made & a certain amount of petrol-economy resulted. The construction & fitting of the Sanitary Section Workshop at Hesru was proceeded with as quickly as possible for Sanitary fittings are urgently required for Township.	

Army Form C. 2118.

WAR DIARY
or
INTELLIGENCE SUMMARY.
(Erase heading not required.)

Place	Date	Hour	Summary of Events and Information	Remarks and references to Appendices
	January 10th		In consultation with D.A.D.M.S. 46th Division & O/C. 168 Mobile Laboratory, re arrangements for direct notification of the Results of tests of Syphilitic cases & for direct notification of syphilitic cases to the A.D.M.S. Office by the R.M.O. concerned. This will we hope help to overcome the difficulty in finding contacts after the notification has come through the Corps. The system of having contacts limited with or prophylactic doses of Anti-syphilitic serum will now cease. In the afternoon saw Col. Hodden O/C 1/3 N.M. Field Ambulance re Syphilitic cases at S. Amand. Particulars and in a letter to A.D.M.S. sent by me on 4.1.17 — a copy of which is in the Appendix.	Appendix B. Appendix C.
	11th		Visited Capt Stud R.M.O. 1st Monmouths re Interim Report in Civilians & sanitation from O/C 8 Mobile Lab. — arranged for further swabs to be taken from the three kitchens and 9 "suspect" cooks. In the afternoon to S. Amand with D.A.D.M.S. 46th Division to see camp site for 138th Brigade Infantry. Difficulties have been encountered here re Ablution accommodation & drinking water for the camp site.	
	12th		To Landinghe & inspected the Sanitary arrangements of village & of R.E. dumps &c.	IV.

A 8834 Wt. W4973/M687 750,000 8/16 D. D. & L. Ltd. Forms/C.2118/13.

Army Form C. 2118.

WAR DIARY
or
INTELLIGENCE SUMMARY.
(Erase heading not required.)

Instructions regarding War Diaries and Intelligence Summaries are contained in F. S. Regs., Part II and the Staff Manual respectively. Title pages will be prepared in manuscript.

Place	Date	Hour	Summary of Events and Information	Remarks and references to Appendices
			Appendix B Plan and Section of Scheme for disposal of Excreta *Section:* Boards with No of day marked; Loose earth; Contents of latrine Bucket; 8'0", 6'0", 2'6" *Plan:* A frame with 12 compartments each 2'0"×1'0" which is filled up with excreta and loamy soil. Trench 9" to latrine. Trench Boards. Compartments numbered 1–24. Ramp to ground level whereon supply of earth is weathered. 13'0", 6'0"	

Army Form C. 2118.

WAR DIARY
or
INTELLIGENCE SUMMARY.
(Erase heading not required.)

Instructions regarding War Diaries and Intelligence Summaries are contained in F. S. Regs., Part II. and the Staff Manual respectively. Title pages will be prepared in manuscript.

Place	Date	Hour	Summary of Events and Information	Remarks and references to Appendices
Alexandria C.			**Pedestal Urinals.**

Elevation — Horizontal Oil Drum cut to form urinal on both sides. Vertical Oil Drums welded to Horizontal Drum to form the pedestal.

Cross Section — Sides of Drum bent vertically to form splash guard. Ground level.

Elevation — Urinal made from biscuit tin. Circular pipe formed with biscuit tin.

Plan — Small perforations. | |

WAR DIARY
or
INTELLIGENCE SUMMARY

Army Form C. 2118.

Place	Date	Hour	Summary of Events and Information	Remarks and references to Appendices
BAINCOURT	30/8/16		Re disinfection on the following day	
do	31/8/16		I went to the South Staffords trenches with the DADMS (any of the 3rd Army) and examined them with the R.M.O. & arrived back at 4 o'clock and attended to office work.	

M. Darling Capt
F.O.C. Sanitary Section
46th Division

3/9/16

WAR DIARY
or
INTELLIGENCE SUMMARY.
(Erase heading not required.)

Army Form C. 2118.

Place	Date	Hour	Summary of Events and Information	Remarks and references to Appendices
Henu.	December 4th		N.C.O's of 46th Divisional Sanitary Section were posted to Town Majors at the following villages for Sanitary Duties:	
			Bienvillers — 2	
			Hongueviller — 2	
			Pommier — 1	
			Souastre — 2	
			Humbercamp — 1	
			Gaudiempré — 1	
			St Amand — 1	
			Henu — 1	
			Warlincourt & Crincourt — 1	
			Pas Huts — 1	
			Grenas — 1	
			A letter was sent by me to each Town Major detailing the duties on which these N.C.O's could be most usefully employed; this arrangement whereby N.C.O's from the Sanitary Section are attached to Town Majors for Sanitary Duties has now been in vogue for a month here and is working very well. When 46th Divisional units evacuated Humbercamp, Bas Huts & Grenas, the N.C.O's concerned were withdrawn.	Off. 7B. III.

Readings 9 a.m.
Appendix C

TOWNSON & MERCER'S
MONTHLY
METEOROLOGICAL RECORD.

Frohen-le-Grand Nov 1st - 2nd
St Riquier " 2nd - 23rd
Frohen-le-Grand " 23rd - 25th
Lucheux " 25 - 30

Station 17th Sanitary Section
46th Division
For the Month of November 1916

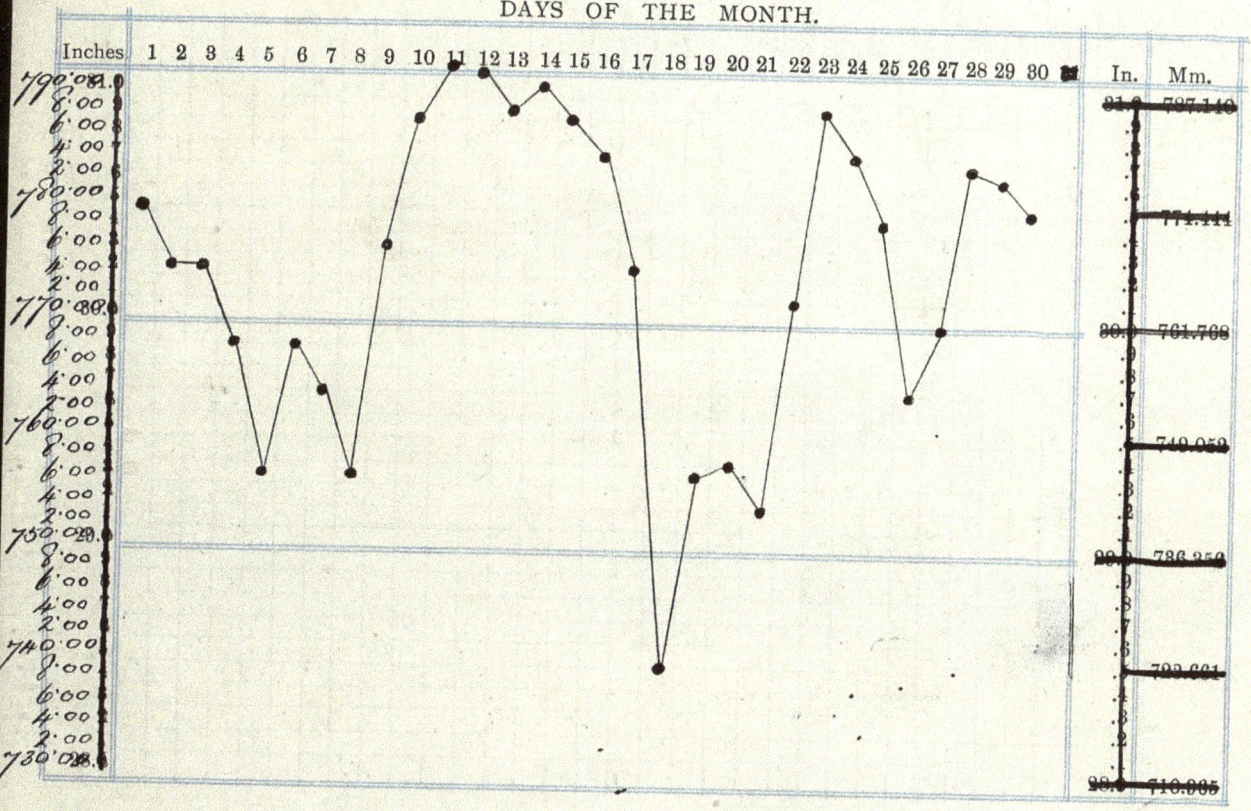

BAROMETER CHART.
DAYS OF THE MONTH.

% of Humidity	Date	Wind Directions	Wind Force	Rainfall	Max.	Min.	Wet.	Dry.	Date	Wind Directions	Wind Force	Rainfall	Max.	Min.	Wet.	Dry.	% of Humidity
92%	1	SE	L	.10	53	42	48	49	17	E	L	.00	43	27	28	30	70%
100%	2	SW	L	.07	69	49	50	50	18	E	M	.00	37	28	30	31	86%
92%	3	SE	L	.10	67	39	47	48	19	SW	L	.47	48	30	30	32	73%
86%	4	SE	L	.09	56	49	51	53	20	SW	L	.00	48	39	42	44	85%
86%	5	S	S	.13	60	30	48	50	21	SE	L	.00	51	32	35	36	91%
100%	6	SW	L	.14	58	47	46	46	22	E	L	.00	43	29	31	32	87%
100%	7	SW	S	.16	53	43	45	45	23	SW	L	.00	48	30	40	42	84%
100%	8	W	L	.65	53	47	49	49	24	SW	L	.00	64	42	41	44	78%
91%	9	W	L	.27	54	40	45	46	25	SW	L	.10	55	46	50	51	92%
86%	10	W	L	.04	53	38	44	46	26	SW	L	.90	59	40	39	40	92%
90%	11	W	L	.00	55	39	47	48	27	SE	L	.08	57	29	32	35	73%
93%	12	NW	L	.01	55	48	51	52	28	SE	L	.01	64	28	32	34	86%
100%	13	N	L	.01	54	48	51	51	29	S	L	.00	44	30	30	31	86%
92%	14	NE	L	.01	54	47	51	52	30	SE	L	.00	32	29	31	32	87%
60%	15	NW	L	.00	55	33	31	36	31	APPROXIMATE amount of Rainfall
86%	16	E	L	.00	44	29	32	34

TOWNSON & MERCER, LD.

Chemical and Scientific Apparatus,  Pure Chemicals Laboratory Outfitters,

34, CAMOMILE STREET, LONDON, E.C.

Place	Date	Hour	Summary of Events and Information	Remarks and references to Appendices
			I am enclosing a weather report for the month showing the maximum and minimum temperatures, the humidity of the air, the reading of an aneroid, the direction and force of the wind and the daily rainfall:- McCartney Capt. r/c Sanitation RE 17th (S) Division	Appendix C

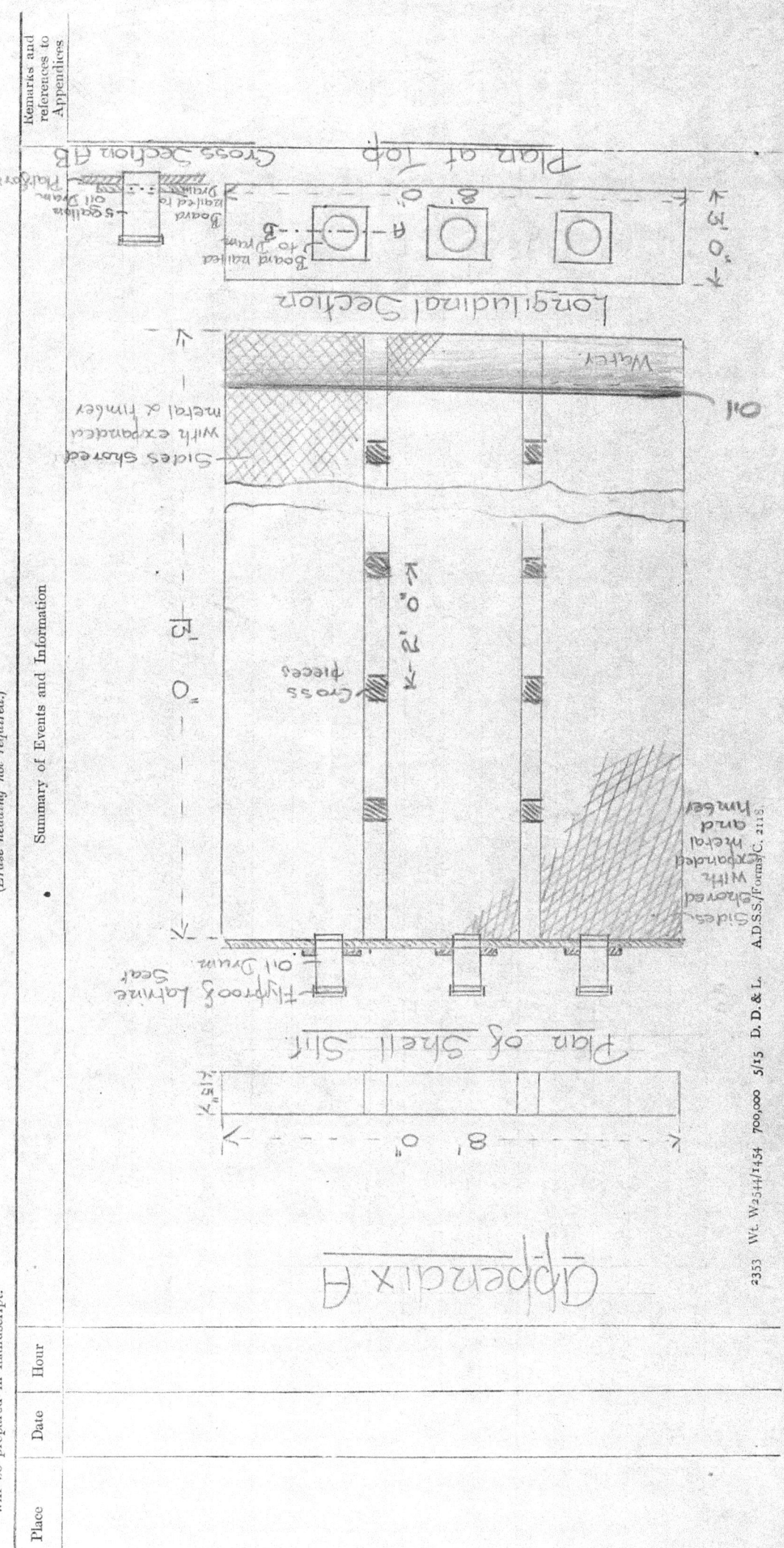

2.

timber & debris. Iron pipes in the well shaft & around the well, suggest that a pump had been used here – recommended to Town Major that R.E's, be consulted as to clearing the well shaft & so making it possible for a sample of water to be obtained. So far this has not been done. In addition to the above, there are two rain water collecting cisterns resembling shallow wells. One of these at K4b.6.2. has a windlass &c. However it is only 15 ft deep & has 3 ft of water in it. There are several cesspools in its vicinity. Notices have been affixed – "For Washing Only".

ESSARTS:- 4 wells.

(1). E 24 d. 9.8.
(2). F 19 c. 2.7.
(3). E 24 d. 8.8.
(4). E 24 d. 8.9.

None of these can be used in their present state as all have been partially destroyed.

It has been impossible to obtain samples up to the present from Wells (1) (2) & (4). A sample was obtained with great difficulty from Well (3.) & proved to be free from chemical poisons & to require ½ Scoop Bl. Powder per W. Cart.

There are two German graves 5 yds or 6 yds from this well. The depth of the well is about 120 ft. I am having the water from this well frequently tested.

This well would prove a useful source of supply of drinking water after repair by R.E's.

Other Wells:- Upon 14:3:17 a letter reached me from M.O., 1/5 Notts & Derby Regt, stating that a well had been discovered in Rattenoy Farm. I wired him to obtain 2 samples for analysis. Upon 15.3.17 I received a note to the effect that the well had been destroyed by shell fire.

A sample was brought to me from Well at Bois Rossignol, K 12 b. 5.4., & was tested:- No chemical poisons detected.
Horrock's Test = 2 Sps Bl. P'd' per W.C.

To my Report to A.D.M.S. 46th Div., upon 19-3-17, I appended the following:- "From the above survey of the conditions of Wells in Gommecourt &c., it is obvious that everything has been done to destroy possible sources of Drinking Water Supply. On account of this I would draw your attention to the imperative need for a thorough overhaul of the Water Carts of the various Divisional Units. Many of these carts have suffered as the result of the recent frost. I would suggest that all C/O's be warned of the difficulties that may arise if the pumps on Water Carts are defective, or if the spare parts are missing from the Carts".

W. Gibbs Capt.
O/c, No. 17 Sanitary Section,

26/3/17.

WAR DIARY
or
INTELLIGENCE SUMMARY.

(Erase heading not required.)

Army Form C. 2118.

Place	Date	Hour	Summary of Events and Information	Remarks and references to Appendices
Henu.	January 1917.		**Infectious Diseases:** Particulars of Infectious Diseases amongst the Civilian Population are those found in the Appendix to this Diary. Amongst the troops in the 46th Divisional Area there were 23 cases of Infections Arising as follows:— Measles: 2 cases in 5th Leicesters Cerebro Spinal Meningitis: 1 case in X 46th Trench Mortar Battery. Diphtheria: 20 cases of those 13 were "Positive" & 7 are suspected cases. Unit: Cases: 4th Leicesters 1 5th " 6 5th Leicesters 3 6th N. Staffs 2 5th N. " 1 6th S. " 1 7th Notts & Derby 1 8th " " 1 1st Mon'mouths 1 11th Siege Batty R.G.A. 1 232 R.F.A. Brigade 1 & 1 Officer R.A.M.C. att. Irish Train. Enclosed is a copy of the Meteorological Report for the month.	Appendix H. W.B.Blis Capt RAMCT a/c 17 Sanitary Section 46th Division. VII.

WAR DIARY
or
INTELLIGENCE SUMMARY

Army Form C. 2118.

Infectious Diseases (contd).

During the period from 20th – 28th Feby when this area was under the administration of 58th Divisional Sanitary Section, there were 12 further cases of Infectious Disease.

5 Diphtheria cases
4 German Measles
1 English Measles
1 Mumps
1 Cerebro-spinal Meningitis.

In my opinion the fact that the 58th Division had just arrived from England & that they arrived in this area well within the incubation period of certain of these infectious diseases would help to account for a certain number of these cases occurring in the Lenn area.

I am enclosing a copy of the Meteorological report for the Month of February 1917.

V. Webbie Capt RAMC.
o/c 17 Sanitary Section
46 Division

Readings 9 a.m.   **TOWNSON & MERCER'S**   Bavincourt
                                              October 1st – 31st
MONTHLY METEOROLOGICAL RECORD.

Station 17^d Sanitary Section
46th Division   For the Month of October 1916

BAROMETER CHART.
DAYS OF THE MONTH.

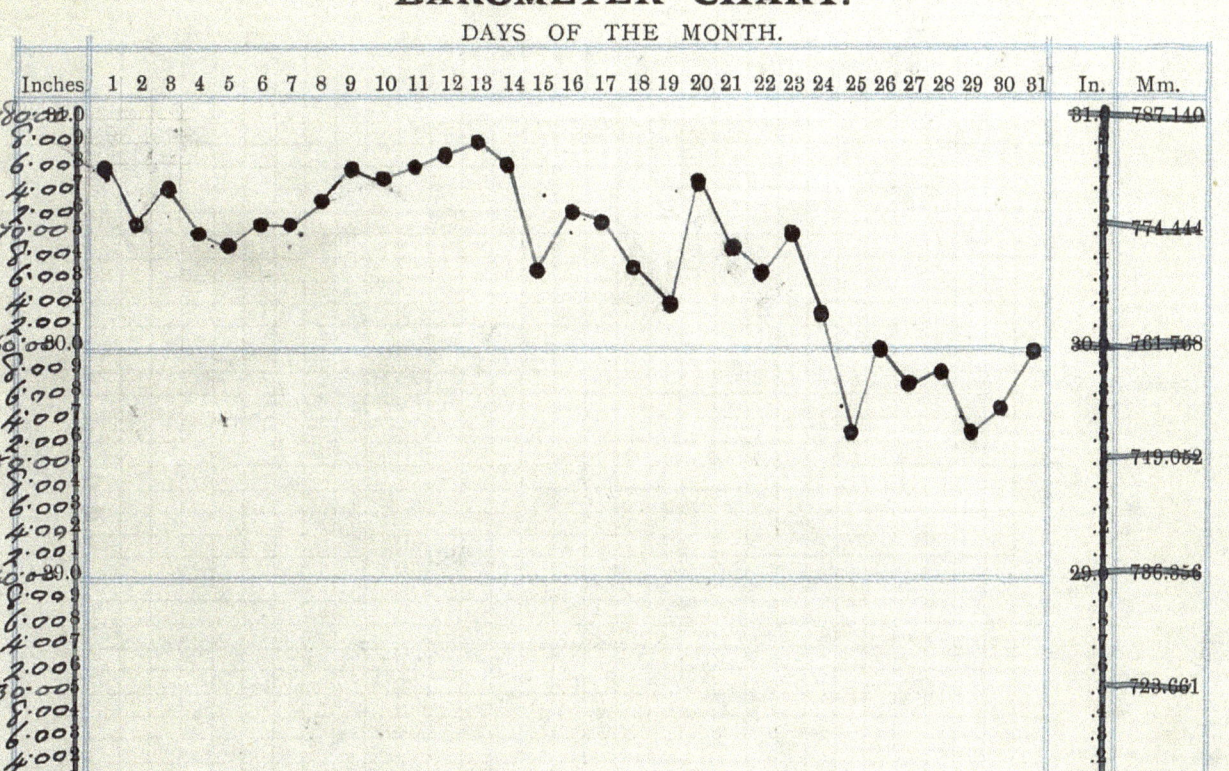

Date	Wind Directions	Force	Rainfall 00/100	Max.	Min.	Wet.	Dry.	% of Humidity	Date	Wind Directions	Force	Rainfall 00/100	Max.	Min.	Wet.	Dry.	% of Humidity
1	NE	L	00	59	47	53	55	86%	17	S	L	10	50	38	47	49	85%
2	SE	L	01	61	47	50	52	86%	18	SW	L	41	54	46	54	54	100%
3	SW	L	68	59	51	55	56	93%	19	NW	L	78	55	47	51	51	100%
4	SE	M	07	65	53	57	57	100%	20	NE	L	08	51	33	34	35	90%
5	S	M	40	63	57	59	61	86%	21	N	L	00	43	28	32	33	89%
6	S	M	10	63	58	60	62	89%	22	E	L	00	43	27	33	34	89%
7	SW	M	10	66	56	55	57	81%	23	SE	L	00	47	35	42	42	100%
8	SW	M	07	61	52	57	58	93%	24	SE	L	22	53	49	47	47	100%
9	SW	M	03	61	51	56	58	85%	25	SE	L	18	51	43	45	46	91%
10	SW	M	00	62	50	56	58	86%	26	S	L	10	50	43	46	46	100%
11	S	L	01	62	52	58	59	93%	27	S	VS	06	50	38	44	45	92%
12	SW	M	04	62	52	58	59	103%	28	S	VS	15	49	44	47	48	92%
13	S	L	00	61	57	57	58	103%	29	SE	VS	02	42	38	43	43	100%
14	SE	L	00	62	54	56	58	89%	30	SE	S	15	51	44	47	47	100%
15	S	L	03	60	53	53	54	93%	31	SW	S	66	55	43	48	51	82%
16	NW	L	04	55	42	44	45	92%									

TOWNSON & MERCER, LD.

Chemical and Scientific Apparatus,      Pure Chemicals Laboratory Outfitters,

34, CAMOMILE STREET, LONDON, E.C.

Flyproof Box Latrine Seat.
For use with Buckets or Deep Trench

Back Rail – To be fixed to ensure lids dropping back over opening

Canvas – To be securely fixed to allow no opening for flies.

Canvas Doors To be of sufficient height to allow of highest pails being withdrawn upright.

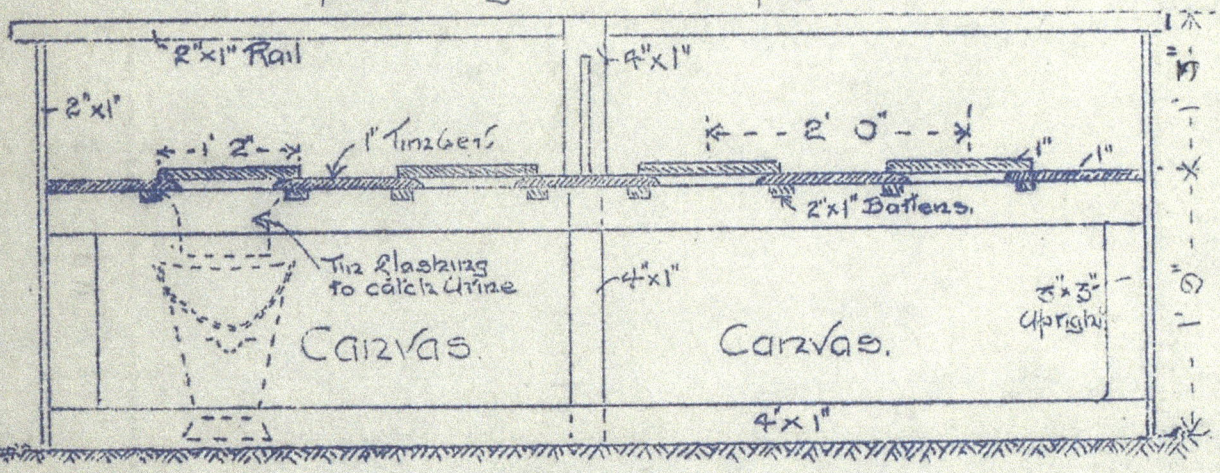

Longitudinal Section

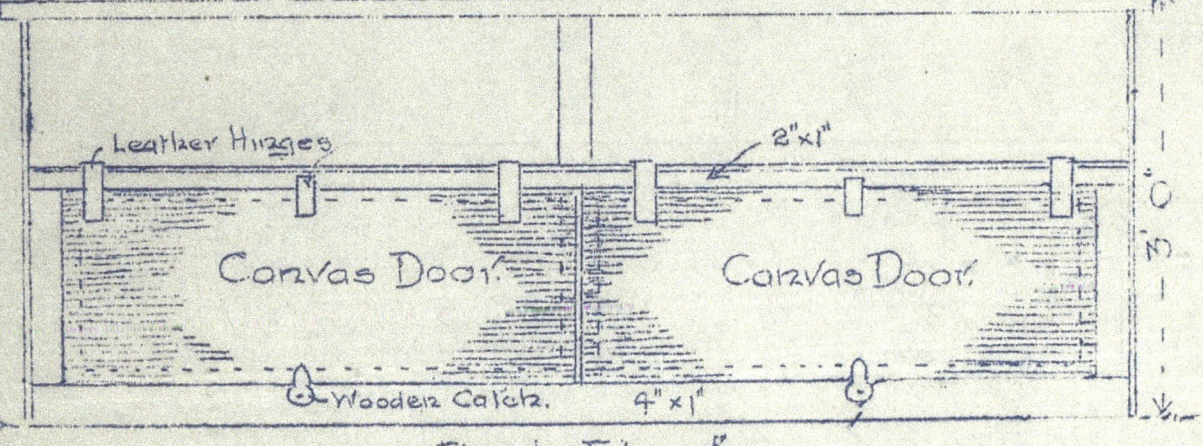

Back Elevation
Shewing door for withdrawing pails

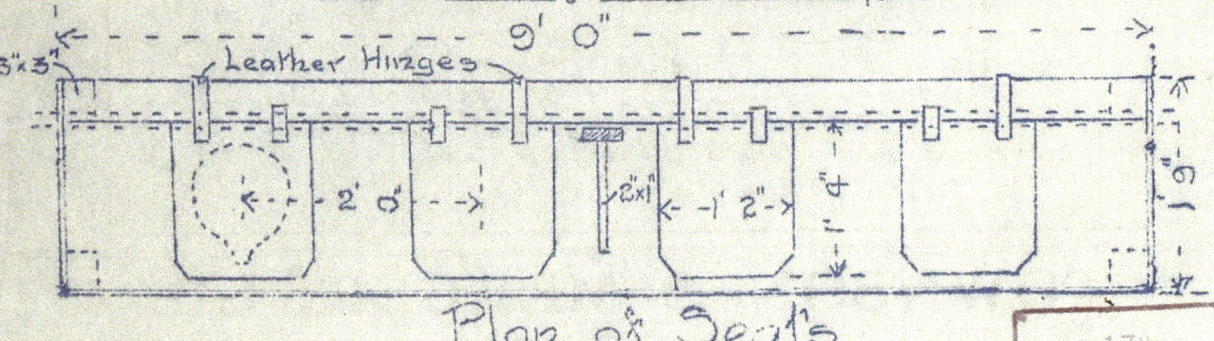

Plan of Seats

17th SANITARY SECTION.

Readings 9 a.m.
Appendix "C"

TOWNSON & MERCER'S MONTHLY METEOROLOGICAL RECORD.

Sept 1st – 30th Ravincourt

Station 17th Sanitary Section 46th Division

For the Month of September 1916

BAROMETER CHART.
DAYS OF THE MONTH.

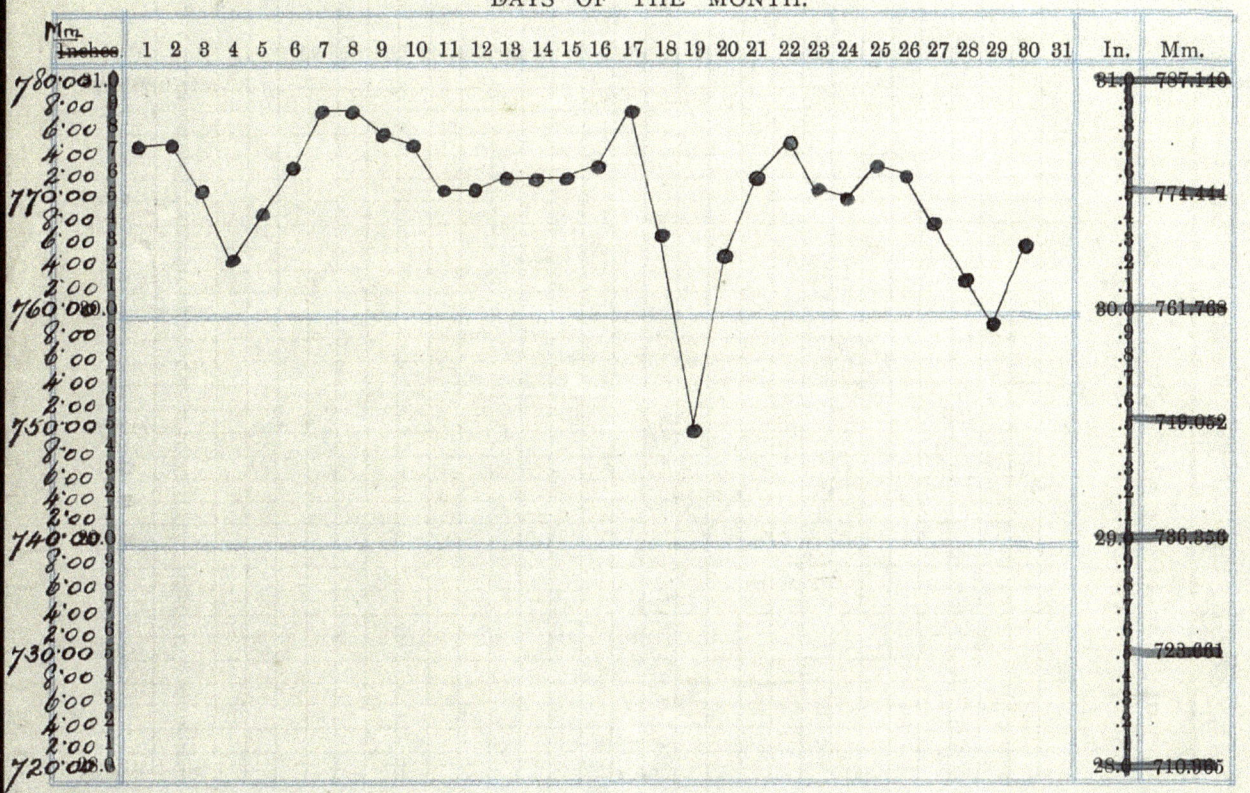

Date	Wind Directions	Force	Rain-fall	Max	Min	Wet	Dry	% of Humidity	Date	Wind Directions	Force	Rain-fall	Max	Min	Wet	Dry	% of Humidity
1	SW	L	.00	65	54	59	60	90%	17	SW	L	.00	60	45	49	51	88%
2	SW	L	.04	68	58	61	62	93%	18	SE	M	.33	62	50	56	56	100%
3	SE	L	.00	72	56	59	61	86%	19	S	L	.97	59	45	46	47	91%
4	SW	M	.27	72	53	54	55	93%	20	NW	L	.23	59	46	51	51	100%
5	W	L	.28	64	49	54	55	93%	21	SW	L	.05	56	49	50	51	93%
6	N	L	.06	57	54	56	57	93%	22	NE	L	.00	57	43	46	47	91%
7	N	L	.00	67	51	55	57	87%	23	E	L	.00	58	43	46	47	91%
8	NW	L	.00	65	56	58	59	93%	24	SE	L	.00	61	47	50	51	93%
9	N	L	.00	69	53	58	59	93%	25	SE	L	.00	65	50	54	55	93%
10	N	L	.00	72	60	60	61	93%	26	SE	L	.00	69	50	54	55	93%
11	N	L	.00	68	55	57	59	86%	27	NE	L	.00	70	54	58	60	84%
12	S	L	.02	66	56	58	60	87%	28	NE	L	.02	68	51	52	53	93%
13	W	L	.05	66	58	60	61	93%	29	NW	L	.13	70	54	59	59	100%
14	NE	M	.03	66	47	49	53	73%	30	N	L	.00	62	52	50	51	93%
15	NW	L	.00	56	40	45	47	83%									
16	NW	L	.08	57	47	56	57	93%									

TOWNSON & MERCER, LD.

Chemical and Scientific Apparatus,  Pure Chemicals Laboratory Outfitters,

34, CAMOMILE STREET, LONDON, E.C.

Readings 9. a.m.

TOWNSON & MERCER'S
MONTHLY
METEOROLOGICAL RECORD.

From 1st to 31st Jan 1917

APPENDIX H.

Station 17th Sanitary Section

For the Month of January 1917

BAROMETER CHART.
DAYS OF THE MONTH.

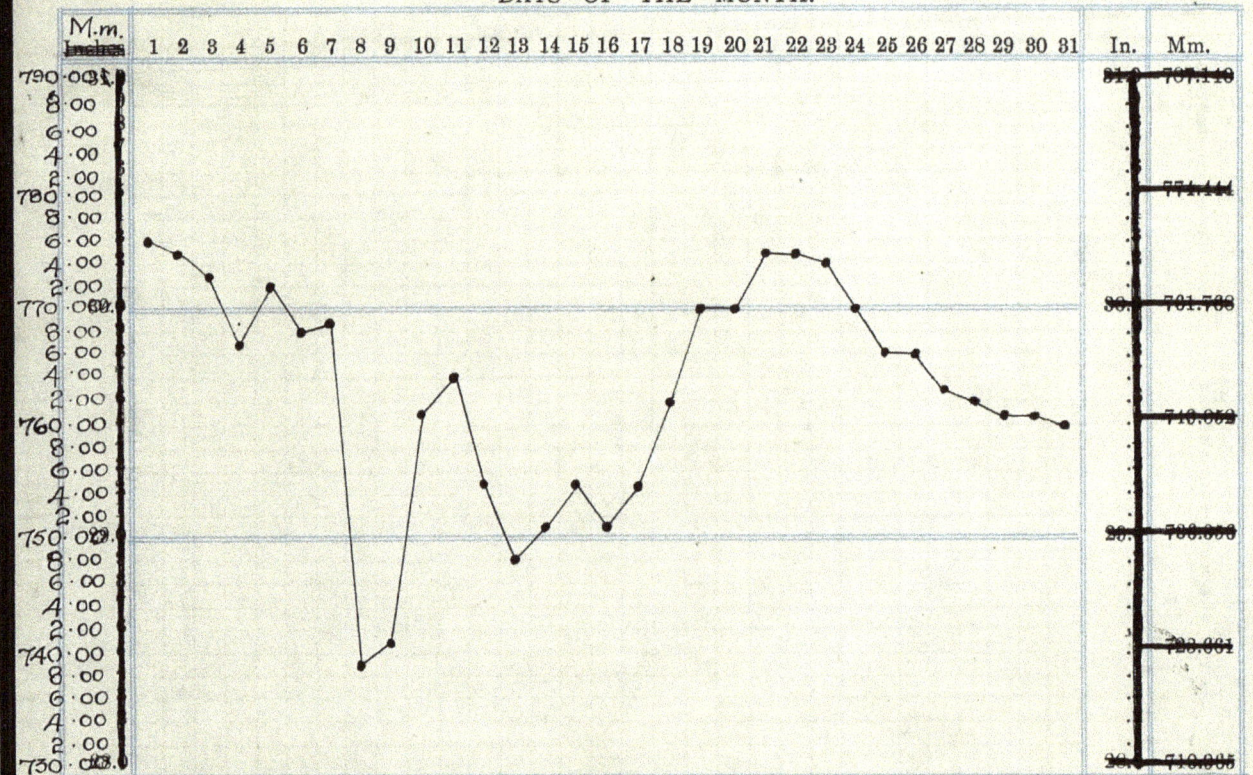

% of Humidity	Date	Wind. Directions.	Force	Rain-fall. .00 /100	Thermometer. Max.	Min.	Wet.	Dry.	Date	Wind. Directions.	Force	Rain-fall. .00 /100	Thermometer. Max.	Min.	Wet.	Dry.	% of Humidity
100%	1	W	L	.12	53	42	47	47	17	N	L	.14※	34	30	32	33	89%
88%	2	W	L	.01	52	43	49	51	18	N.W	L	.05※	37	31	32	33	89%
100%	3	S.W.	L	.02	51	45	48	48	19	N.E.	L	.10※	36	30	30	32	76%
92%	4	S	M	.06	49	45	47	48	20	N.E.	L	.00	36	28	28	29	85%
91%	5	W	L	.14	47	33	37	38	21	N.E.	L	.00	31	28	29	30	82%
91%	6	W	L	.32	47	33	39	40	22	N.E.	L	.00	31	29	30	31	86%
73%	7	S.W	L	.00	44	30	32	35	23	N.E.	L	.00	36	17	18	20	48%
91%	8	S.W	M	.52	44	35	39	40	24	N.E	L	.00	41	14	17	19	46%
73%	9	N.W	L	.14	50	34	32	35	25	N.E.	L	.00	42	14	17	19	46%
82%	10	N	M	.01	39	33	35	37	26	N.E.	L	.00	43	12	18	20	48%
89%	11	N.W	L	.00	46	32	32	33	27	N.E.	L	.00	34	14	18	20	48%
91%	12	W	L	.14	45	32	37	38	28	N.E.	L	.00	42	16	19	21	50%
90%	13	W	L	.21※	44	32	34	35	29	N.E.	L	.00	43	11	⊕	16	Reading Unobtainable
89%	14	S.W	L	.12※	35	33	33	34	30	N	L	.00	44	14	18	20	48%
89%	15	N	L	.00	39	32	32	33	31	N	L	.04※	38	18	21	22	71%
73%	16	N	L	.00	38	30	29	31				※ Snow.			⊕ Thermometer Frozen.		

TOWNSON & MERCER, LD.

Chemical and
Scientific Apparatus,

Pure Chemicals
Laboratory Outfitters,

34, CAMOMILE STREET, LONDON, E.C.

Readings 9.am.

TOWNSON & MERCER'S
MONTHLY
METEOROLOGICAL RECORD.

Lucheux. Dec. 1st – 6th.
Henu. Dec. 6th – 31st.

Station **17th Sanitary Section** 46 Division

For the Month of **December** 1916

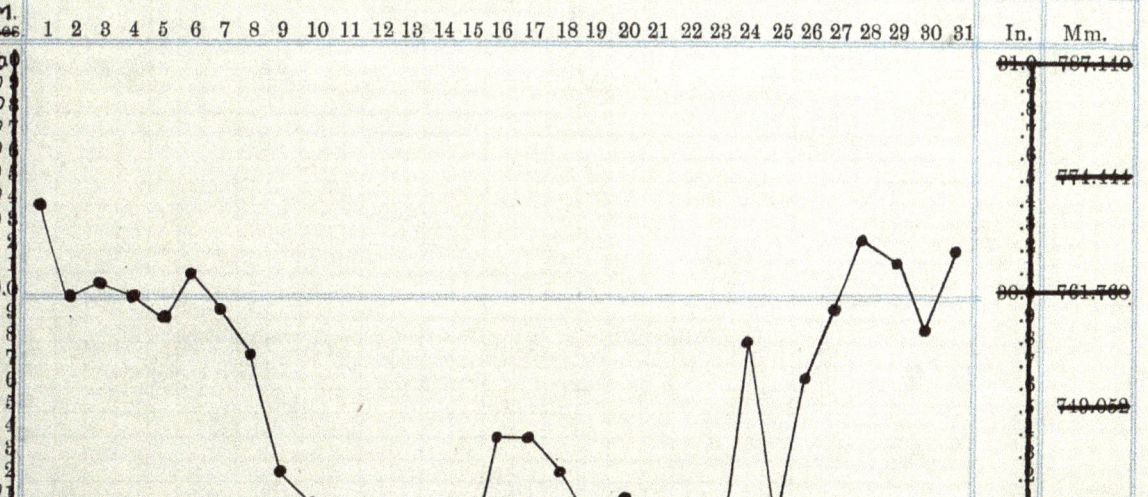

BAROMETER CHART.
DAYS OF THE MONTH.

Date	Wind. Directions.	Force	Rain-fall. 00/100	Max.	Min.	Wet.	Dry.	% of Humidity
1	S.E.	L.	.00	34	29	31	32	87%
2	N.E.	L.	.00	34	28	29	30	83%
3	N.E.	L.	.00	32	29	31	31	100%
4	N.E.	L.	.00	35	27	31	32	87%
5	W.	L.	.02	62	34	36	37	91%
6	S.E.	L.	.11	50	31	37	38	91%
7	N.W.	L.	.00	43	33	33	34	90%
8	N.E.	L.	.06	38	34	37	38	91%
9	E.	L.	.10	40	38	39	39	100%
10	E.	L.	.45	42	32	37	38	91%
11	S.E.	L.	.05	41	31	35	37	83%
12	N.E.	L.	.41	49	31	31	33	78%
13	S.W.	L.	.06	37	34	36	37	61%
14	S.E.	L.	.12	39	31	36	37	91%
15	E.	L.	.13	39	35	37	38	91%
16	S.W.	L.	.16	40	31	32	33	88%
17	S.E.	L.	.01	38	32	31	32	87%
18	S.W.	L.	.03	36	32	32	34	81%
19	S.E.	L.	.00	35	29	29	31	73%
20	S.E.	L.	.00	34	29	30	32	73%
21	E.	M.	.01	44	28	36	37	91%
22	S.	L.	.31	43	35	39	39	100%
23	S.E.	M.	.42	51	35	51	51	100%
24	S.W.	L.	.20	53	35	38	39	91%
25	S.W.	S.	.21	52	36	44	45	92%
26	S.E.	L.	.15	48	33	38	39	91%
27	N.	L.	.19	52	32	37	38	91%
28	S.E.	L.	.00	58	28	31	33	78%
29	S.	L.	.35	49	33	49	49	100%
30	S.W.	S.	.92	52	46	47	47	100%
31	S.W.	M.	.01	52	42	47	48	96%

*Snow.

TOWNSON & MERCER, LD.

Chemical and Scientific Apparatus,

Pure Chemicals Laboratory Outfitters,

34, CAMOMILE STREET, LONDON, E.C.

Deep Trench Latrine
Flyproof Cover

Trench - To be 12'0" x 4'0" x 10'0" deep
Rail - To be fixed to ensure lids dropping back over opening
Foot Guides To be 1" strips 9" long 6" apart & to be at angle of 30°
Lids - To have at least 1½" overlap on opening all round.

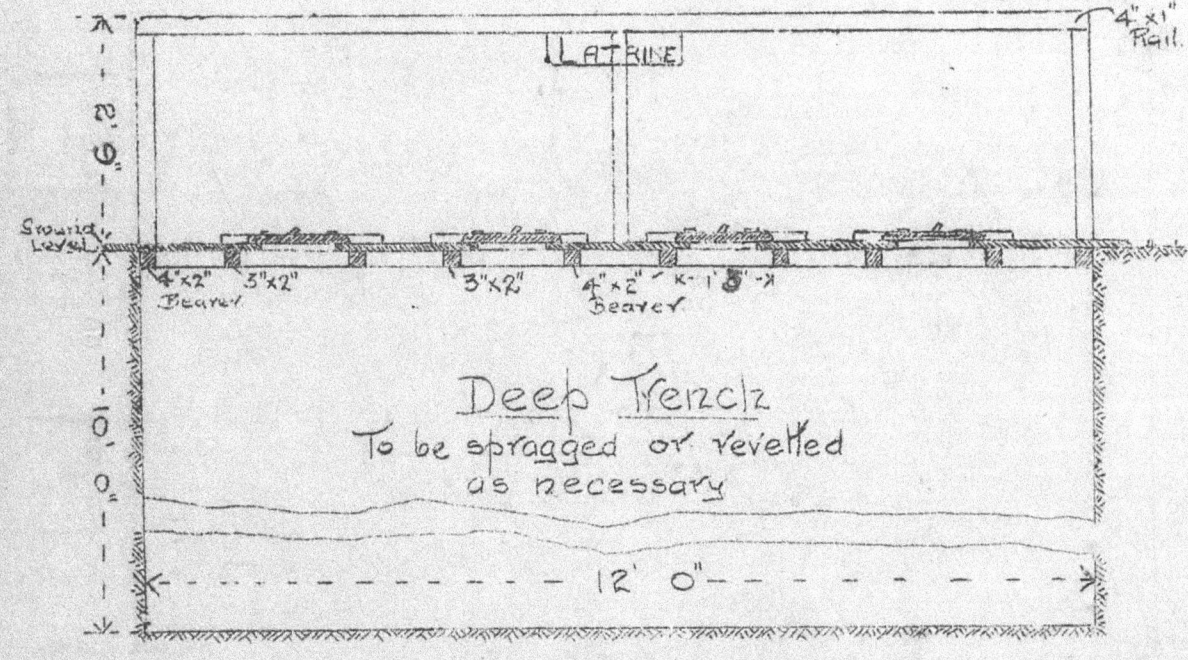

Longitudinal Section

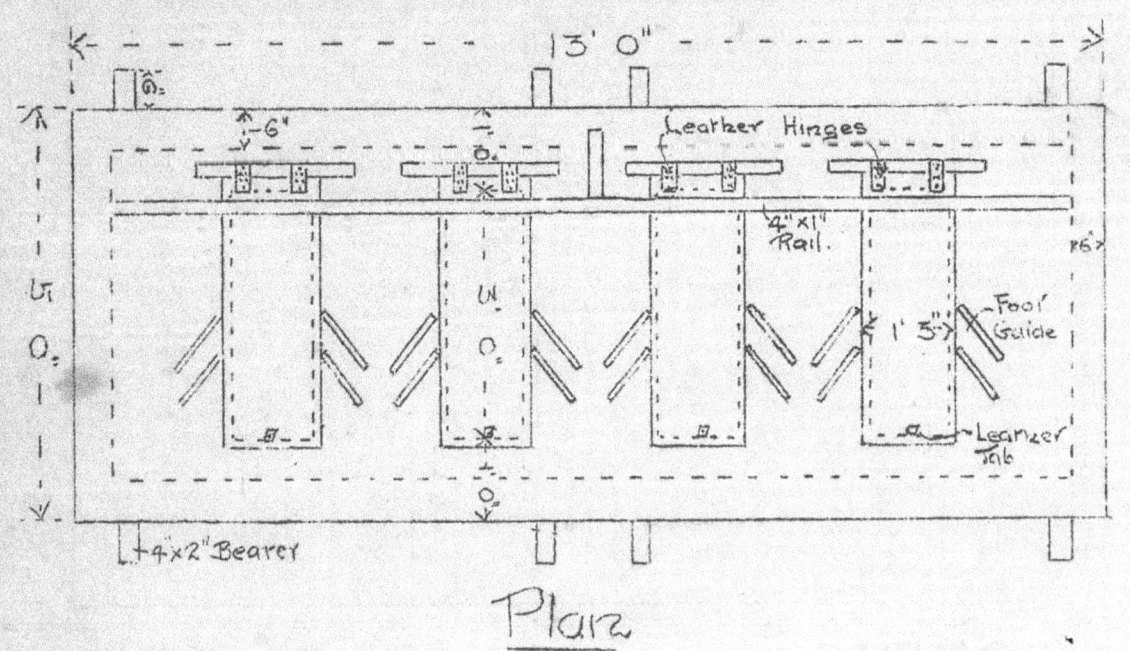

Plan

17th SANITARY SECTION

To:- A.D.M.S. 46th Division

From:- O/C No 17 Sanitary Section 46 Division

Report on Water-supplies for Gommecourt.

APPENDIX. B.

GOMMECOURT   As the result of a thorough inspection of Gommecourt area by Sgt. Addison of this Sanitary Section, three wells have been discovered as follows.

(a) Map ref. E.28.C.15.5. It was not possible to obtain a sample of water from this well owing to obstructions.

(b) Map ref. E.28.C.9.2. This well is 180 feet deep but is dry and the brick-work has been partially destroyed.

This well I understand, was previously reported to you by O/C 1/2nd N.M. Field Ambulance as requiring 2 scoops Bleaching Powder per cart. It would seem that since it was previously tested there has been an extensive fall of the sides of the structure with the result that the well is now dry.

(c) K.4.a.8.8. This well is almost full of debris and had evidently been used to carry away the effluent from the adjacent baths.

In addition to the above, there are two rain-water collecting cisterns somewhat resembling shallow wells.

One of these at K.4.b.6.2. has a windlass. It is 15 feet deep with three feet of water in it. There are several cesspools in the vicinity of this cistern.

There are therefor no sources of drinking-water supplies in Gommecourt itself. However, a careful survey of

1

TOWNSON & MERCER'S MONTHLY METEOROLOGICAL RECORD.

Readings. 9 a.m.
February 1st–26th HENU
" 26–28 Gouy.

Station 17" Sanitary Section 46" Division

For the Month of February 1917

BAROMETER CHART.
DAYS OF THE MONTH.

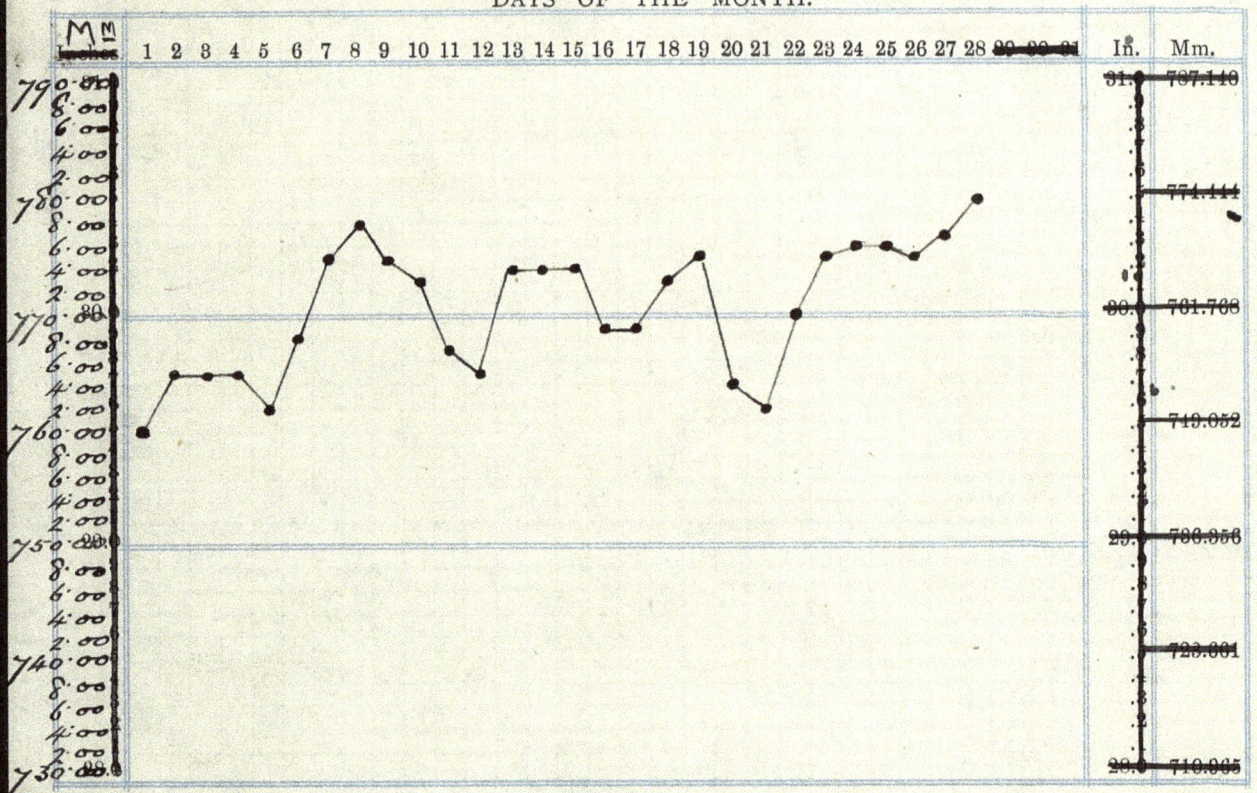

% of Humidity	Date	Wind. Directions	Force	Rain-fall.	Max.	Min.	Wet.	Dry.	Date	Wind. Directions	Force	Rain-fall.	Max.	Min.	Wet.	Dry.	% of Humidity
71%	1	N	L	.00	35	18	21	22	17	SE	L	.03	40	31	38	39	92%
71%	2	N	L	.00	34	19	21	22	18	SW	L	.08	44	36	38	38	100%
67%	3	N	L	.00	43	11	19	20	19	SE	L	.00	41	33	36	37	90%
67%	4	N	L	.00	48	9	18	19	20	W	L	.10	39	34	36	36	100%
53%	5	NE	L	.00	46	14	22	24	21	W	L	.03	40	36	38	38	100%
71%	6	NW	L	.00	39	10	21	22	22	W	L	.05	44	36	39	40	92%
67%	7	NW	L	.00	20	13	19	20	23	W	L	.04	40	33	35	36	90%
70%	8	N	L	.00	25	13	20	21	24	W	L	.00	41	31	34	35	96%
66%	9	N	L	.00	30	10	14	15	25	SW	L	.00	39	32	37	38	91%
47%	10	NE	L	.00	29	10	16	18	26	NW	M	.03	48	42	42	43	93%
73%	11	NE	L	.00	33	20	23	24	27	NW	L	.00	56	40	45	47	86%
56%	12	N	L	.00	31	17	19	21	28	W	L	.00	45	37	41	42	93%
87%	13	NE	L	.00	36	29	31	32									
77%	14	NE	L	.00	36	21	25	26									
71%	15	NE	L	.00	34	22	25	26									
87%	16	NE	L	.00	37	22	31	32									

TOWNSON & MERCER, LD.

Chemical and Scientific Apparatus,  Pure Chemicals Laboratory Outfitters,

34, CAMOMILE STREET, LONDON, E.C.

Water Report. (cont'd)

The water-supply in Fonquevillers enabled me to recommend to Capt. Wheatcroft of the 139th Infy Brigade a way out of the difficulty.

The Wells in Fonquevillers are as follows:-

1) Map Ref E.27.a.1.0. — 2 scoops B. Powder per cart
2) " " E.27.a.2.3. — 1 scoop " " "
3) " " E.27.a.9.6. — 1 scoop " " "
4) " " E.21.b.4.9. — 1 scoop " " "
5) " " E.27.b.7.3. — 1 scoop " " "

(These wells were all tested by Sgt Addison upon 8/3/'17).

Well 1). E.27.a.1.0. is behind Town Major Office. A 5-h.p. petrol engine has now been fixed at this well and a pipe conducts the water to the street. Here carts may be filled. A notice is being prepared at the Sanitary Section workshop and will be fixed stating the chlorine value of the water. i.e. 2 scoops per cart.

" 2). E.27.a.2.3. is at the Advd Dressing Station and is in use.

" 3). E.27.a.9.6 is opposite the Church.

" 4). E.21.b.4.9. is near the Gendarmerie.

" 5). E.27.b.7.3 is at the last billet on the Gommecourt Road on the left.

4) and 5) were previously under observation and so were little used.

It is suggested that a pump similar to that at Well No.1 be installed at Well No.5 and so lessen the tendency to overtax Well No.1. If need be, a pipe could be laid from Well No.5 to a service cistern in Gommecourt later.

The quality of the water in Well No.5 is good and only requires 1 scoop B. Bleaching Powder per cart.

2

Appendix D.

<u>Report on Baths. Gommecourt</u>
(Sketch plan attached)

The old German Baths are in a cellar Map reference E.28.d.4.1.

These baths have a system of 4 large sprayers which discharge over a cement lined pit 7′ × 7′ × 4′ approximately.

The water is drawn from a rain-water cistern at the rear of the cellar and empties into a cement tank in the bath-room.

The boiler is a shallow Iron tank of about 100 gallons capacity built over a brick fire-place. To this tank the sprayers were connected. One of the connecting pipes has however been removed.

There is no outlet at the bottom of the cement lined pit. The waste water has apparently been pumped from the pit in the small chamber at the side. From there the waste water is piped into a man-hole and finally discharged into a well near the road.

One corner of the roof has been knocked in, and part of the debris has fallen into the pit.

M. Gebbie. Capt RAMC
o/c No 17 San. Section

22.III.17

Reading 9. a.m.   Appendix F.   March 1st–31st Menu

TOWNSON & MERCER'S
MONTHLY
METEOROLOGICAL RECORD.

Station 17th Sanitary Section

For the Month of March 1917

BAROMETER CHART.
DAYS OF THE MONTH.

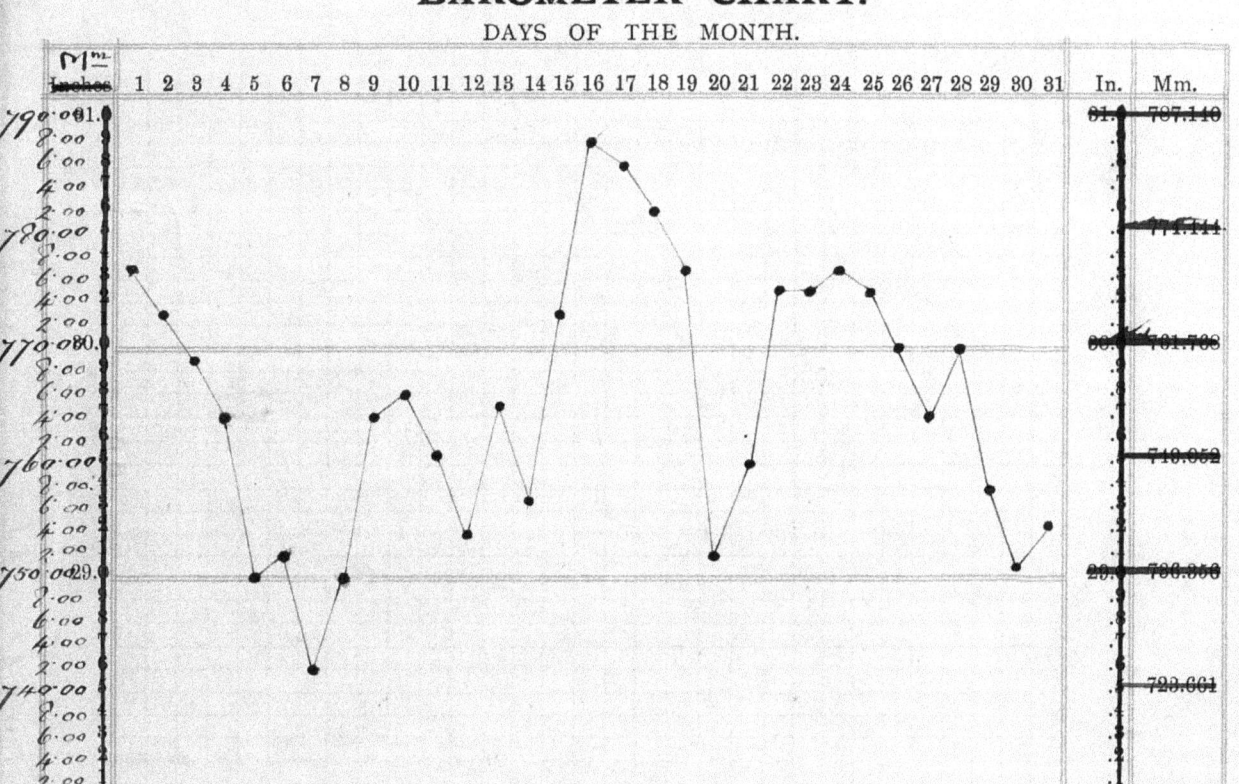

Date	Wind. Directions	Force	Rain-fall	Max.	Min.	Wet.	Dry.	% of Humidity	Date	Wind. Directions	Force	Rain-fall	Max.	Min.	Wet.	Dry.	% of Humidity
1	W	L	·03	46	39	41	42	92%	17	SW	L	·00	50	33	40	41	92%
2	NW	L	·00	34	26	31	33	78%	18	W	L	·00	54	35	41	42	92%
3	N	L	·00	46	28	31	32	87%	19	SW	L	·00	56	37	41	41	100%
4	E	L	·00	39	27	29	32	76%	20	W	S	·46	49	34	35	35	100%
5	E	L	·21	41	30	32	33	89%	21	N	M	·11	44	32	31	32	89%
6	E	L	·02	48	32	37	40	77%	22	N	M	·07	40	27	32	32	100%
7	NE	S	·00	51	31	31	32	87%	23	NE	S	·67	43	26	32	33	89%
8	NW	S	·00	34	24	30	32	76%	24	NW	S	·60	42	26	30	31	86%
9	SE	M	·00	34	24	31	32	87%	25	NE	M	·00	42	27	34	35	90%
10	SE	L	·09	40	31	37	38	91%	26	NW	L	·27	52	36	36	36	100%
11	SE	L	·02	47	37	44	45	92%	27	NW	M	·67	50	31	33	34	89%
12	S	M	·37	57	44	47	48	92%	28	SW	L	·04	44	27	30	30	100%
13	SE	L	·21	52	39	40	41	92%	29	SE	S	·10	54	35	41	42	92%
14	SW	M	1·05	52	39	42	43	92%	30	S	L	·31	49	36	42	43	92%
15	NW	M	·07	50	32	35	35	100%	31	S	M	·06	47	33	37	37	100%
16	NW	L	·00	47	29	29	30	82%									

TOWNSON & MERCER, LD.

Chemical and Scientific Apparatus,  Pure Chemicals Laboratory Outfitters,

34, CAMOMILE STREET, LONDON, E.C.

Appendix B.

To:- Town Major Lucheux

From:- O.C. Sanitary Section 46 Division

Reference Huts at LUCHEUX at present
occupied by R.E. (Labour Batt.) } 10 huts
1st Monmouth Regt (Pioneers) }

I visited the above huts and the
camp site this morning and I have to
submit the following recommendations

(a) That a new Urine pit be dug. filled
with burnt tins and rubble. Oil
drums and petrol tins for same will
be supplied from the Sanitary Section
Stores. A suitable site for new
Urine pit is close to existing latrines
on the incinerator side of same.

(b) That the existing urine pit be closed
and the site marked.

(c) That the Incinerator be mended.
Earth removed from back of same
to free draught hole. Bricks to be
pointed in mortar or puddled clay.

(d) That a Sanitary fatigue man should be
selected to attend to the incinerator
for stoking etc.

Latrines

(e) That the present latrines be used.
Oil drums be supplied in place of
the existing petrol tins and bresol
used instead of Chloride of Lime.

(f) That the refuse from the latrines be
removed daily to the incinerator
and burnt.
The Sanitary Section will supply
12 Oil drums for these latrines.
These oil drums to be fitted with
wire handles before being used.

APPENDIX B.

R.A.M.C. Circular Memorandum N° 81.

O's C Field Ambulances
All R.M.O's.

Owing to the increasing number of Diphtheria cases occurring in the Division, the following procedure will be adopted in every case, including suspected cases:—

The billet will be placed out of bounds and disinfected.

All immediate contacts isolated, Throat Swabs taken by R.M.O. distinctly marked and forwarded with a Nominal Roll shewing Regt. N°. Rank. Name. Regiment and Division specifying diphtheria contacts, to Field Ambulance concerned for transmission to Mobile Laboratory.

Throat Swabs will be obtained from the Mobile Laboratory, kept in stock by Field Ambulances and issued to R.M.O's as required.

Officers Commanding Field Ambulances will send swabs for examination direct to the Mobile Laboratory.

Prophylactic dose of Anti-diphtheritic need not be given to contacts if this procedure is carried out.

If a case is diagnosed as Suspected Diphtheria in a Field Ambulance, the O.C. Field Ambulance will notify the R.M.C concerned, who will then act as above.

If contacts are found to be negative, they can be released from quarantine — if positive, they will be sent to the Field Ambulance

D.

To:- A.D.M.S.   46 Division
From: O/c 46 Div Sanitary Section.

Today I inspected Billet 34 at LUCHEUX and found that this billet was until recently, used by 46 Div. R.A. as Officer's Mess.

In the yard, I found a heap of rubbish. This rubbish looked very old for the most part but on the top, were fresh tea leaves, potato peelings and tins.

From reports received just before we left the LUCHEUX area I find that the 46 Div. R.A. had started to clear away an accumulation of rubbish left by 30th Div. R.A. and had the billet itself cleared out.

This work was proceeding when the 46 Division left the area, and it is to be regretted that it was not satisfactorily continued after the supervision of the Sanitary Section was withdrawn.

I beg to suggest
(1) That the pile of cinders in Billet 34 be used for garden paths.
(2) That the refuse pile be collected and burnt. (arrangements to be made with 49th Div. Sanitary Section for this to be done.)
(3) That the necessary steps be taken to prevent a recurrence of this by bringing the matter to the notice of the C.R.A. 46 Division.

W Gibbie Capt.
O/c 46 Div Sanitary Section

23/12/16

APPENDIX G.

To:- O/c French Mission. 46th Division.
From O/c 17th Sanitary Section. 46th Division

Interim Report on outbreak of Measles at HENU.

My attention was first drawn by French Mission 46th Division to the presence of civilian cases of Measles in HENU on January 13th 1917.

There were 3 cases in a house in D Road near billet No. 26, involving the members of one family - ANCELIN by name. The necessary precautions were taken to prevent the spread of the disease and preliminary arrangements made to have the bed clothes, etc disinfected in due course.

Further cases were notified on January 23rd and a sharp decline in School attendance was reported to me on the same date by the French Mission. The notified cases were visited the same day and treatment and precautionary measures instituted.

On January 24th by kind permission of the School Master I inspected the children attending school and, as several of the children there shewed premonitory symptoms, I decided to ask for the closure of the school for a period of 14 days from the day of onset of the last recorded case. i.e. January 22nd. This has been done.

As the result of a house to house inspection of all civilians in HENU, I have now to report that there are 15 cases of Measles amongst the civilian children between the ages of 6 and 14 years.

11 houses are involved and there are 18 contacts amongst children of school age.

I am arranging to visit the cases and the

To - D.D.M.S.   V.th Corps

Report on Water Supplies at FONQUEVILLERS, GOMMECOURT and ESSARTS.

Part of the subject matter of this report viz. that part referring to GOMMECOURT and FONQUEVILLERS has been already reported upon by me to A.D.M.S 46th Division upon 9th March 1917.

Since then, the investigation has been extended and the results up to date are embodied in this report.

APPENDIX C.

FONQUEVILLERS. Wells in Fonquevillers that can be used are:-

1. Map ref E.27.a.1.0. - 2 scoops Bl. Powder per cart.
2. " " E.27.a.2.3. - 1 scoop " "
3. " " E.27.a.9.6 - 1 " "
4. " " E.21.b.4.9 - 1 " "
5. " " E.27.b.7.3 - 1 " "

At 1 a 5 h.p Petrol Engine has been fixed and a pipe is conducted from the well to the street where carts, lorries etc may be filled. Two tanks are placed here and the end of the pipe rests in one of these tanks. Notices have been affixed at all these wells.

Up till the evacuation of GOMMECOURT by the Germans, wells 4 and 5 were under observation and were little used. I recommended to A.D.M.S 46th Divⁿ the fixing at 5 of an apparatus similar to that at 1 above described so that the drain on the supply at 1 would not be too severe, but, so far, this has not been considered necessary.

GOMMECOURT.   4 Wells.

1. - E.28.c.3.5 - Sample not obtainable owing to obstructions.
2. - E.28.c.9.2 - 180 feet deep - brick work partially destroyed. Well is dry.
3. - K.4.a.8.8 - This well is full of debris. It had probably been used to carry away the effluent from the adjacent baths.
4. - K.4.a.7.9 - approached from a dug out - The top of the well is obstructed by

(g) That the existing refuse pit be filled in and the new one to be now used for clinker and burnt refuse from the incinerator.

(h) That the chimney of the kitchen requires repairing

(i) That the existing Ablution benches be well scrubbed

(j) That a Soap Trap be fixed between the Ablution benches and the soakage pit.

(k) That the existing soakage pit be partially filled in with rubble and tins.

(l) That the straw from the soap trap be burned daily in the Incinerator

(m) That some of the burnt tins from the incinerator be used for footpaths to the latrine, incinerator etc.

Should the Town Major desire it a N.C.O. from this Section can be detailed to supervise the fatigue party in carrying out the above work

W. Gibbie. Lieut. R.A.M.C.(T)
29/11/16   of 46 Divl Sanitary Section

A.

To:- Town Major. Lucheux

From:- O/C 17th Sanitary Section 46 Division

Further Recommendations re Huts at LUCHEUX.

I am pleased to find that your fatigue party has started work on the Sanitation of the Huts occupied by R.E's, and Monmouths. The work proceeds satisfactorily.

Re The Huts at present occupied by the R.F.A (30th Division).

Recommendations

(1) That the camp site be cleared of waste paper, and the rubbish that has been scattered about.
That the rubbish heaps be cleared away.

(2) That the existing latrines be improved (on lines) similar to those for the other huts.

(3) That the existing urine pit be used, that the drums and urine receptacles be renewed, and raised to a suitable height to prevent splashing.

(4) That Ablution benches be made, and a soap box and a soakage pit be introduced.

(5) That the kitchen sheds be improved, the kitchens cleaned and the grease burned in the fire.

Oil Drums for latrines and urine pit will be supplied by the Sanitary Section as before.

W Geblie Lieut.

1/12/16

O/C 46th Div. Sanitary Section

Measles cases (Civilians) at Henu.   APPENDIX F.

To A.D.M.S. 46th N.M. Division.
From O/C 17 Sanitary Section, 46th Division.

Notification having been recieved from the French Mission of an outbreak of Measles amongst the Civilians at Henu, I have, today, personally visited all the cases notified & have inspected the Billets &c. concerned.

Billet in D. Road near French Mission (no number.)
 3 Cases: Ancelin Georges, 14 yrs
   " Germaine, 7 yrs
   " Hector, 2½ yrs.
These cases I first saw upon 13.7.17 in consultation with Capt Shanks of D.A.C.
   One other child in family Albert aet 10 yrs.
   No troops billet at this house, nothing sold to troops & no washing done.
   23.7.17 All these cases have improved & are out of bed.
Children do not go to school & isolation is maintained.

Billet 26: Lallart Omer, aet 11 years,
   & Lucienne Delalle, aet 11 years,
are suffering from Coryza. — No rash yet visible.
   Koplick's spots not seen.
   Both cases have been Measles contacts at school.
   Children are being kept away from school.
   No troops at this billet.

Billet 21: "C Mess"
   Irene Derwiller, aet 7 years, — Measles.
   Last at school on 13.7.17 — onset of illness 14.7.17
The following Officers have their mess at this billet.
   Capt. Bailey, Lieuts. Fisher, Eddowes, Barrs & Richards.
The cooking is done in an outhouse but the servants have bought Eggs, milk &c from the civilians concerned.
   Two of the officers Lieuts Fisher & Eddowes sleep in a room adjoining the mess.

Billet in D. Road — Georges Ancelin 14 yrs
near No 26. — Germaine "   7 yrs
             — Hector   "   2½ yrs

Billet No 26 — Lucienne Lelalle 11 yrs

No 21 — Irine Servilles 7 yrs

No 29 — Marcellin Candilier 11 yrs

No 34 — Michel Biterne 7 yrs

No 62 — Lucien Candaes 6 yrs
        — Marie   "   8 yrs
        — Leon   "   10 yrs

"   No 22 — Ferdinand Bucquet 7 yrs

"   No 50 — Alfred Louchet. 7 yrs

Billet near chateau — Raymond Gaudon. 6½ yrs

No 55 — Florine Noiret 10 yrs

Billet in C Road — Jennie Leclercq 7 yrs
near No 55

VERY URGENT.

APPENDIX
D.

O.C.,

        Regt.

Will you please supply me
with the following information.
Please give reply in column
of remarks.

REMARKS.

1.   Position of Manure Heaps.
       Map references.

2.   Method of transporting
       Manure to Dumps.

3.   State the number and kind
       of carts used.

4.   Where the carts are obtained
       from, i.e. if belonging to
       Unit or local farmers etc,.

5.   Are these carts used for any
       other purpose, if so, what ?

                    J.R.U. Maughan
                    Major. D.A.D.M.S.
               for A.D.M.S. 46th. Divn.

21/1/y

APPENDIX C

To:- A.D.M.S.   46th Division

The following cases of Diarrhœa have occurred recently among men of the 137th Brigade Depot at ST AMAND.

Nominal Roll of cases referred to.

No 20024   Pte VAUGHAN /5th North Staffords.
No 5558   Pte HAMISHAW.S. 1/6th North Staffords.
No 4568   Pte JENNINGS.F. 1/6 North Staffords.
No 3283   Pte THACKER. N /5 South Staffords.
No 20027   Pte WORTHINGTON.E. /5 North Staffords.
No 20541   Pte MATKIN. R. /5 North Staffords.

Colonel Hodder of 1/3rd N.M. Field Ambulance drew my attention to these cases and we decided to await the report from o/c 2nd N.M. Field Ambulance of their condition before taking a more serious view of the matter.

This report has now come to hand stating the cases are of mild type, and that similar cases are reaching the Field Ambulance from other areas.

I am arranging for the water used by these troops to be carefully chlorinated, and am recommending to o/c 1/3rd N.M. Field Ambulance that no further precautions at present need be taken.

W. Webbe Capt.

7/1/17.   o/c 46th Div. Sanitary Section

Spot Map - Civilian cases of Measles.

HENU

Appendix E.

Sketch Plan of Old German Baths Gommecourt

Appendix E.

III.

In view of these facts, I propose to take the following precautions.

1. Take steps to have the school closed for a period of 14 days from the time of onset of the last case. i.e. from 22nd January 1917.

2. Have all the billets marked "Out of Bounds to troops."

3. Have all contacts civil & military isolated & medically examined daily for 14 days from 22nd. I. 17.

4. Stop all sale of foodstuffs to the soldiers by the civilians concerned.

5. Arrange for the disinfection of clothing (soldiers') at present at Billet 29.

With regard to "C Mess", I think it would be advisable to carry out Isolation & examination of the Officers concerned & their servants. This would apply more especially to the cases of Lieuts Fisher & Eddowes who slept near the mess.

23.I.17.

W Gillie
Capt.
O/c. 17 San. Sectn.
46 Division

E.1

To:- A.D.M.S.   46th Division
From:- o/c 46th Divl Sanitary Section.
Re: C.R.A. cookhouse behind chateau at HENU.

There is a large accumulation of rubbish including tea leaves and tins near the cookhouse just vacated by the 49th Divl C.R.A.

Arrangements have been made for this to be removed.

The cookhouse itself is very dirty and I have suggested that it should not be used.

At SOUASTRE the billets vacated by the 49th Divl Artillery were left in a very dirty condition. This has been reported to the Town Major who has taken the matter in hand.

W Gebbie. Capt.

23/12/16.   o/c 46th Divl Sanitary Section.

B. To:- Town Major.

I have today sent L/Cpl ———
of this Section to be attached to
you for the following Sanitary duties.
(1) To inspect the Village and report
on any insanitary conditions
found therein.
(2) To report on the state of the roads.
(3) To report on the state of billets
left by units.
(4) To report on vacant billets.
(5) To inspect wells and report on
their condition.
(6) To supervise fatigue parties working
on the roads, cleaning billets,
attending to public urinals,
latrines, ablution benches and
incinerators.

W. Hebbe Capt.

7/12/16   /46th Divl Sanitary Section

11.

Billet 29: Marcelline Candilier, aet 11 yrs. Measles.
Last at school 17.7.17.
Headache " 13.7.17.
No troops billeted here but washing for troops is done. I am arranging for this to cease & for the clothing at present on hand to be disinfected before re-issue to the owners.

Billet 54:
Michael Aiterne, aet 7 yrs. — Measles.
Last at school 17.7.16.
Onset 19.7.16.
No troops billeted here but "B" mess servants get milk from this farm.

Billet 62:
Candais. Lucien, aet 6 years. Measles — rash faded.
Last at school 16.7.17. Onset 16.7.17.
Candais. Marie, aet 8 years. — Measles.
Last at school 16.7.17. Onset 22.7.17. (rash).

Candais. Léon, aet 10 years. — Measles.
Last at school 16.7.17. Onset 22.7.17.

Other children in the house — Ernest 16 yrs - has had measles.
Paul. 14 yrs. - has not had measles.
Lucienne. 13. " " " "
Raymond. 3. " " " "
Casimir. 1 yr. " " " "

No troops billeted here but some of the men of R.E. Signals come occasionally for coffee.

Drawings of Drying Room and Incinerator existing on site of 3rd N.M. Field Ambulance at CAUDIEMPRÉ.

Scale ½ Inch to 1 Foot.

APPENDIX. A.

Plan

Walls 5" Thick composed of mud and straw between 2 sheets of expanded metal

- Covered shed for men stoking incinerator
- Bars
- Sliding door
- Drying Room
- Dump for refuse
- 10'-0"
- 14'-0"

Longitudinal Section.

- Plate for excreta
- Incinerator
- Bars
- Rack for clothes
- Support
- Oil drum flue
- Foot cap

Water Report (cont'd).

General observations: From the above survey of the conditions of wells in Gommecourt it is obvious that everything has been done to destroy possible sources of water-supply. On account of this, I would direct your attention to the imperative need for a thorough overhaul of the water carts of the various Divisional units. Many of these carts have suffered as the result of the recent frost. I would suggest that all C/O's be warned of the difficulties that may arise if the pumps on water carts are defective or if the spare parts are missing from the carts.

W. Hebbie Capt.
I/c N° 7 Sanitary Section
46th Division

9th March 1917.

contacts and to have the houses involved placed "out of bounds" to the Troops.

The bedclothing etc will be disinfected later.

Appended is a list of names of children involved and of the houses in which the cases have occurred.

A. Gebbie. Capt.
of 46 Divl Sanitary Section

26/1/17.

Result of Bacteriological examination will be notified to R.M.C's from this office. Disinfection of billets etc. will be carried out by the Sanitary Section.

Every case of infectious or suspected infectious disease will be immediately notified to this office by the R.M.C. concerned, giving particulars as stated on pro-forma attached.

(Signed). J. St. A. Maugham.
Major. D.A.D.M.S.
for A.D.M.S. 46 Division

10/1/17.

(Roll No. 11.) W.O.O. Sanitary Section

October 1916

COMMITTEE FOR THE
MEDICAL HISTORY OF THE WAR
Date -5 OCT. 1916

(No 1) 46th Divisional Sanitary Section

COMMITTEE FOR THE
MEDICAL HISTORY OF THE WAR
Date 4 APR 1917

w095/2681/3
1897/5004

9140/1158

4th Division

19th Sanitary Section

Oct 1916

COMMITTEE FOR THE
MEDICAL HISTORY OF THE WAR
Date −2 DEC. 1916

140/94/1.

46 L Div.

No. 14 Sanitary Section.

COMMITTEE FOR THE
MEDICAL HISTORY OF THE WAR
Date 13 MAR. 1917

140/1246

(No. 14) 46th Divl. Sanitary Section

Nov. 1916

COMMITTEE FOR THE
MEDICAL HISTORY OF THE WAR
Date −3 JAN. 1917

COMMITTEE FOR THE
MEDICAL HISTORY OF THE WAR
Date 26 OCT 1916

140/2043.

46th Div.

No. 17.
th Div. Sanitary Section

March 1917

COMMITTEE FOR THE
MEDICAL HISTORY OF THE WAR
Date 11 MAY 1917

140/900

COMMITTEE FOR THE
MEDICAL HISTORY OF THE WAR
Date 31 JAN. 1917

(No 17) 46th Divl. Sanitary Section

Disease or Suspected Disease	Regt No Rank & Name	Unit	Coy	Plat.	Billets Localization No of House and map reference	Date when Billets in previous Column were occupied 18 days previous to day of Onset	Date Billets in previous Column were vacated	Date sent to Field Ambulance or Hospital	Nºˢ & Names of Contacts	What Contacts Isolated	Sanitation of Billets	Remarks re: any possible source of infection

www.ingramcontent.com/pod-product-compliance
Lightning Source LLC
Chambersburg PA
CBHW081550160426
43191CB00011B/1889